PENGUIN BOOKS

Journey *of a* Thousand Storms

Kooshyar Karimi was born in Tehran and now lives in Sydney. He is the author of several books on Iranian, Chinese and Assyrian myths and history, one of which was banned from publication by the Iranian government. His memoir *I Confess: Revelations in Exile* was published in Australia in 2012, and his bestselling book *Leila's Secret* was published by Penguin in 2015. He is an award-winning translator of Gore Vidal, Kahlil Gibran and Adrian Berry, among others.

T0362945

ALSO BY KOOSHYAR KARIMI

I Confess: Revelations in Exile

Leila's Secret

Journey
of a
Thousand
Storms

KOOSHYAR KARIMI

PENGUIN BOOKS

PENGUIN BOOKS

UK | USA | Canada | Ireland | Australia
India | New Zealand | South Africa | China

Penguin Books is part of the Penguin Random House group of companies
whose addresses can be found at global.penguinrandomhouse.com.

Penguin
Random House
Australia

First published by Penguin Random House Australia Pty Ltd, 2016
This edition published by Penguin Random House Australia Pty Ltd, 2017

10 9 8 7 6 5 4 3 2 1

Cover design by Louisa Maggio © Penguin Random House Australia Pty Ltd
Text design by Laura Thomas © Penguin Random House Australia Pty Ltd
Cover photographs: mountains by Wolfgang Zwanzger/Alamy Stock Photo;
storm clouds by STILLFX/Shutterstock; man and child by InesBazdar/Shutterstock
Typeset in Adobe Caslon Pro by Penguin Random House Australia Pty Ltd
Colour separation by Splitting Image Colour Studio, Clayton, Victoria
Printed and bound in Australia by Griffin Press, an accredited ISO AS/NZS 14001
Environmental Management Systems printer.

National Library of Australia
Cataloguing-in-Publication data:

Karimi, Kooshyar, author.
Journey of a thousand storms / Kooshyar Karimi
9780143786092 (paperback)

Karimi, Kooshyar.
Jews, Iranian – Biography.
Physicians – Iran – Biography.
Refugees – Iran – Biography.
Refugees – Australia – Biography.
Human rights – Iran.

penguin.com.au

To Newsha, Niloofar, Anna and Jonathan

For our journey

ONE

The bus I'm in is about to cross the border from Iran to Turkey – from my beloved home to an unknown land. I feel simultaneously exhilarated and ashamed. Nobody should have cause to feel happy about permanently fleeing their homeland, ever. I am alone in every sense. My wife crossed the border separately, with our two daughters, six hours ago. Azita is a Muslim and can go to Turkey freely. I'm Jewish, and I am the one they want.

At five in the morning the bus stops at Tabriz, the town on the border. This is the last checkpoint, the last stop in Iran. All the passengers give their passports to the customs officer and for the next two hours we wait for our names to be called. People are excited to be going to Turkey, to a land that allows them to listen to Western music and to dance and drink alcohol without being persecuted, but my reasons for being in this bus are very different.

I pace up and down outside the immigration office, chain-smoking. I try to stay calm by telling myself, Get ready to be shot, don't be scared, death is nothing to be afraid of. When my name is finally called, my heart races even faster and my palms are wet. I try to hide my tense expression, but no mask can cover a man's dread when he's tossing a coin for life or death. Although in many ways death would be a blissful relief, I'm still frightened. I haven't enjoyed my life so far but I'm worried about my daughters. I don't want them to grow up without a father.

But miraculously, the Iranian border officer hands me back my passport, duly stamped. Not having the slightest clue what's going on in my terrified mind, he gestures to me to move on. A voice inside me whispers, *You are free. You can go.* But I cannot. I am transfixed. I turn my head and glance at the mountain through the window. This will be the last time I see Zagros, the summit on which ancient Persian heroes fought with evil forces to protect our land. Farewell, my Iran! Goodbye, my beautiful home, I say to myself, and force myself to leave the office.

I step onto the Turkish side of the border in a state of shock. My joy is so intense and my sorrow so profound that I can hardly breathe.

'Welcome to Turkey,' says a Turkish police officer. Despite his fake formal smile, these three simple words immediately become the loveliest of lyrics.

When I join my family later that day, at a bus stop halfway to Istanbul, they hardly recognise me. I can barely contain my emotions, nor can my older daughter, Newsha, when she finally realises that the malnourished ghost smiling at her is her father. I've lost so much weight I look like a dead body pulled out of hot sand. This is the first time I've seen my younger daughter, Niloofar, who was born while I was on the run. She has big black eyes, plump lips and a gorgeous smile. I hold her in my arms and whisper, 'I will never leave you again. Never.'

The bus to Istanbul passes through villages with satellite dishes on every roof. I am struck by the contrast with Iran, where you are arrested if you attempt to watch foreign TV. Big Brother doesn't want you to know what's going on in the outside world. Marrying someone not approved of by your parents or criticising the Supreme Leader are also serious crimes, as is a woman allowing a few strands of hair to show from under her scarf. These laws are based on what the Prophet Mohammad dictated fourteen centuries ago and are upheld by old men who have no idea about modern technology or civil rights, men who are intolerant of any form of change because it makes them disoriented. That's why Iran isn't progressing, and why there are innumerable reasons to be publicly hanged there: homosexuality, blasphemy, adultery, apostasy, or, God forbid, questioning the Prophet Mohammad's decision to allow his nine-year-old daughter, Fatima, to marry his 25-year-old cousin, Ali. Iran has one of the highest rates of execution in the world. In my homeland, expressing curiosity is like wandering blind through a minefield.

I have made no plans beyond reaching Turkey and have no idea what the next step will be. I know I'm far from safe even here, as the Iranian and Turkish governments regularly exchange political prisoners and dissidents. Fugitives like me disappear in this country every day. But still, I have never been so thankful – I am alive.

I can't stop looking at my daughters. Five-year-old Newsha is asleep on her seat, and baby Niloofar is quietly lying on Azita's lap. I sip Scotch from the bottle I bought at the Turkish border, silently celebrating my escape.

As the bus winds its way through the unfamiliar countryside, the significance of what I've done really hits me for the first time. There can be no turning back from here. And I can't help thinking about everything that's led me to this point.

It began, in a way, while I was in primary school, on my birthday in 1978. My mother, father, brother and I were sitting at home in Tehran listening to BBC radio for the latest news about the revolution. My father had borrowed the transistor radio from Reza Frekans, his friend who owned an electronics repair shop. I didn't have a birthday party or get any presents. Celebrations, trips to the cinema, shopping – these belonged to fairytales. Where I lived, in the basement of a house in the slums, the most joyful moments were having a full stomach or surviving typhoid. Moreover my father, a bus driver with three wives and seven children, hardly even remembered my name, let alone how old I was.

Nevertheless that birthday turned out to be exceptionally important. For several months there had been demonstrations against the Shah. During his reign the elite had devoted themselves to amassing wealth, while the rest of society was increasingly devoted to the rewards of religion. The Shah's biggest mistake was to underestimate the mullahs' influence on the masses. Now, in a last effort to retain control of his country, the Shah had declared a military curfew: anyone outside after dark would be shot on sight. Despite this, the streets were full of protesters marching and chanting slogans.

It was seven in the evening and we could hear sporadic gunfire. My mother was praying in Hebrew under her breath for the bloodshed to stop, but my father was furious that the majority of young Iranians were against the Shah. 'Our country is now very prosperous and these idiots are going to destroy it,' he announced, glaring at the radio.

I had never seen my father so frustrated, but what mattered most to me was that he was there, with us, on my birthday. He visited only once or twice a month, and every night I prayed for him not to have an accident on the notoriously dangerous roads. I now worried about what would happen to him when he left the next day. The previous week some revolutionary guerrillas had fired at his bus, shattering the windshield and the side window, narrowly missing his forehead.

A bang on our door startled us. 'Don't open it,' said my father.

After a moment of tense silence the banging resumed, louder and faster. 'It could be the army or police,' said my mother. 'If we don't let them in they'll smash the door.'

My father got up. 'You stay here,' he ordered us.

He opened it carefully. To his astonishment a young man stood there panting and shaking. 'Please let me hide in your house —' he began, but was interrupted by a close round of heavy gunfire.

'Get out of here,' said my father, going to shut the door.

'Baba jan, please . . .' I murmured from behind him, and my mother added, 'Be kind, Khalil. He will be shot if we don't help him.'

My father shook his head. 'I don't care,' he said.

The man told us he had been taking part in a peaceful demonstration when the army rushed in and opened fire. 'I saw dead bodies everywhere,' he said. 'A tank ran over a woman and crushed her chest.'

I imagined him slipping on his own blood on the street. Suddenly I had an idea. 'Let me hide him in the bus, Baba jan.' I pulled my father's sleeve.

'Kooshyar is right, let him hide in the bus. Please,' begged my mother.

My father looked at me and finally said, 'Okay.'

'Thank you, sir,' said the young man. 'May Allah bless you and your family.'

I sprinted to the bus, the key in my fist. I knew this key very well – my father would give it to me whenever he came home from remote parts of Iran. I'd sweep the floor between the forty-three seats, inhaling dust from deserts, and if I found an old coin it would make my day. Most times, though, there'd only be a plastic bag full of vomit, so I'd fetch the hose and a bucket and wash the whole bus. When I finished, my father would smile, give me a rusty, crooked coin (the equivalent of about twenty cents) and say, 'Good boy.' I'd run to the grocery shop with the coin in my hand feeling rich and happy, convincing myself, *My father cares about me. He loves me.*

But it was my mother who starved herself to feed us, who comforted us when we were afraid and who suffered in abject poverty. She did her best to shield my brother, Koorosh, and me against harm and disease, sacrificing her life so we would be safe and educated.

I led the protester to the bus, where I grabbed another key from the glovebox and opened the luggage compartment. There was just enough room for two slim people. I slipped in and lay down.

'Get in,' I said to the terrified man. 'Yallah! Shut the door!'

The darkness was absolute and smelled of diesel and old rubber. I felt the man's breath on my cheek, and the cold metal under my back. Neither of us dared speak. We could hear tanks rumbling in the street, some shouting and the occasional gunshot.

After ten minutes we heard soldiers being ordered to check the nearby houses and narrow lanes. My heart thudded in my throat and I was drenched in sweat. The protester remained silent, breathing deeply and trying to keep still. I was more worried for him than for me: the soldiers were unlikely to shoot a kid. But would they punish my family? Would they kill my father for letting a fugitive hide in his bus?

Now there was banging on doors in our street. I had experienced fear many times in my life by then, but nothing this intense, this crushing.

'If they catch me I'll tell them I kidnapped you and forced you to hide me here,' the man whispered. His words soothed me but a few minutes later I heard my father say nervously, 'Here, officer.' We listened as the bus door was opened and then footsteps of soldiers, maybe two or three, were right above our heads. I stopped breathing, waiting for them to come and search the luggage compartment. I wanted to run out and shout, 'I'm innocent!' I felt a strong hand grasping my wrist; it seemed that the man had read my mind and was trying to calm me down. In the midst of my fear I admired his courage.

Eventually, the footsteps retreated, but we lay there in the cramped space for another half an hour, until we were sure the soldiers had gone. It took a long time for my breathing to return to normal.

'What is your name?' the man asked as we waited.

'Kooshyar,' I whispered. 'What's yours?'

'Ali Mazaheri. Kooshyar, you are a brave boy. Thank you.'

Once the tumult in the streets had settled I opened the compartment door and we crawled outside. Ali said, 'Kooshyar, I owe you my life,' and then he slipped quietly away.

Seven years later I was about to sit my final exams when a *sardar*, a chief commander in the army, came to our school. Iran had been at war with Iraq for five years by then, with more than a million people killed. Four hundred students gathered in the hall to meet the war hero, and when he finally arrived we stood and clapped for a long time. But it was not his large black eyes, well-trimmed beard, square jaw and impressive height that struck me, nor his passionate speech urging us to join the fight against Iraq. I recognised the commander instantly. He was the revolutionary I had hidden in my father's bus.

Eight years after that I was an intern in Imam Reza Hospital, doing my last year of medical training. One morning I went to check on a patient after his surgery and saw the name on his file. It was Ali Mazaheri. He'd been given strong sedatives following a third operation to remove shrapnel from his spine. I put my hand on his shoulder to wake him and when I told him who I was he smiled.

'Kooshyar,' he mumbled.

But it was the fourth and final time I met Ali Mazaheri that had the most profound impact on my life. In May 1999 I had been on the run from MOIS, the Iranian intelligence service, for three months, hiding in remote towns on the Caspian coast. Following torture I had been forced to become a spy for them, and had gathered information that led to the arrests of many people, including thirteen Jews accused of being spies for Israel. The regime had issued a death sentence for them, and I knew that with my mission now complete, I was the next target.

The arrest of the thirteen Jews had caused an international outcry. The United States Congress, the European Union and the United Nations demanded that Iran release the prisoners, but none of this would help me. My homeland was no longer safe, but I had no passport and no money to pay people smugglers to get me across the border.

Before fleeing to the coast I'd bought a fake birth certificate in downtown Tehran, in the notorious slum where I was born. I didn't have much time. If MOIS were to find me they would tear my body to pieces. They had told me this often enough.

My only chance was Ali Mazaheri, who was now in charge of the passport office. Would he save me? Or would he turn me in? According to Middle Eastern tradition, we had become brothers that day on the bus twenty years ago, but I had no idea whether Ali would respect the code of brotherhood, whether he'd remember telling me he owed me his life.

I came out of hiding and went to Ali Mazaheri's office, even though I knew that by doing so I was risking both our lives. As soon as he recognised me and saw my expression, he understood the graveness of my situation and agreed to meet me somewhere safe. When he appeared he was wearing a hat and sunglasses. I told him I had to leave Iran and needed a passport.

After a painful silence he took off his sunglasses, inhaled deeply and quietly asked me if I had a photo and my details written down. I handed over the information, which he put into his pocket. Ali studied my face and I saw something in his eyes that day, something I hadn't seen in them for twenty years. It was fear.

I tried hard not to tremble or break down. Then Ali grabbed my hand in his sweaty grip.

'Pick it up tomorrow, same place,' he said at last. I wanted to hug him but I just nodded.

As I walked away he said, 'Don't ever come back, Kooshyar, or I will be hanged.'

The next day I had the fake passport with a note: *You have only forty-eight hours.*

TWO

The bus stops in the middle of the night at a restaurant a few hours from Istanbul. I need to pee. I've almost finished the bottle of whisky and I feel euphoric. This is the first time I've consumed a commercially made alcoholic drink. Up until now, if I wanted to drink I had to make wine at home using my mother's traditional Jewish recipe, a crime punishable by ten years' jail, or else buy it on the black market: enormously expensive homemade vodka that was ninety percent industrial ethanol mixed with water.

I go to the toilet and find out I have to pay the equivalent of two dollars to use it. This is unbelievable to me – toilets are free in Iran. I find some scrubby bush and urinate there instead. My drunken state transforms the cries of crickets into opera. I join my family in the restaurant and the prices on the menu also startle me. Ten dollars for a sandwich! I ask Azita how much money she has managed to bring with her.

'I have seven million toman from selling the car, so close to four thousand dollars in total.'

'If only we could sell our house,' I sigh, thinking about all we have left behind. Azita glares at me and I can read her mind: This is all your fault. I try to comfort her by saying, 'Even if they take the house, at least the children still have a father.'

We eat a piece of bread and drink some water before going back to the bus. When Azita changes Niloofar's nappy the other passengers complain, whispering 'Evsiz.' I don't know a single Turkish word, but the meaning of this one is clear enough.

At five in the morning we arrive in Istanbul, a crowded, raucous city of almost nine million. I ask around to find out where the cheap part of town is and a taxi driver takes us to Aksaray. He wouldn't take his European customers to such a noisy, polluted area. The language barrier is a concern but we assume we'll spend just a few days in Turkey, until we get a visa to another country.

I'm impressed by the number of women with uncovered hair in the streets, walking or driving European cars. After all, Turkey is a Muslim state too. Just fifteen hundred kilometres to the east, many Iranians are living in conditions akin to the Dark Ages. We see a few people who look like Iranian tourists. Night-life does not exist in Iran except inside the soundproof houses of super-rich *hajis* in uptown Tehran, where the police can be bribed.

Checking into the hotel is difficult without speaking Turkish, but we manage to get a small room and settle in. There is no air conditioning and it is the middle of a hot and humid summer. My shirt sticks to my skin. I turn on the tap in the bathroom, pour water on my head and drink several glassfuls. Newsha passes out in front of the TV and Niloofar eventually falls asleep on Azita's lap. I'm astonished to learn that Turkish TV has more than thirty-five channels. In Iran we have only three: two for giving bad news and one for praising the Supreme Leader.

While Azita and I count our remaining money, I try not to dwell too much on our situation. I'm only thirty but until recently was established as a doctor, with my own practice. I was also a well-known author and an award-winning translator. I'd completed my two years' compulsory military service. I had a nice Peugeot and no debts.

That life collapsed when I was kidnapped by MOIS. They had three reasons: I was a Jew pretending to be a Muslim, I was writing a book about the history of Jews in Iran, and as a doctor I'd helped women who had been raped, or who'd fallen in love outside marriage, by terminating their pregnancies or restoring their virginities, thus preventing them from being murdered by male family members or being stoned to death by the government's Revolutionary Guards. Any one of these offences was enough to have me executed. I know how lucky I am to have escaped.

Our luggage holds some of my books, a shirt, a picture of my favourite desert in Iran, and four thousand American dollars. This hotel room costs forty dollars a day, and already I have some idea that other living expenses for the four of us in Istanbul will be at least fifty dollars a day. This means that, including the price of a visa and plane tickets, we don't have much time to get to a safe country. I try not to feel anxious. After facing torture and imminent death at the hands of MOIS, just being alive and outside Iran feels like paradise.

In the middle of the night I wake with abdominal cramps, and so does Azita. Newsha follows, screaming in pain, and Niloofar too begins moaning. Food poisoning, I think. But we haven't eaten out; we couldn't afford it. I go downstairs to get some help and the receptionist says, 'Silly Iranians. You can't drink tap water in Istanbul.'

'So how do we get water?'

'You have to buy it,' he says, laughing,

I pay two dollars for two bottles of water and go back to our room to find Azita vomiting. Even the most rural communities in Iran have drinkable water. I begin to doubt the prosperity of the Turkish people.

After a restless night we set off for the Israeli embassy; I'm confident they will support us because I'm a Jew. Azita is reluctant to move to Israel but nevertheless we take a taxi to the other side of town. Although the trip is very expensive – twenty-two dollars – I'm excited. We are going to Israel, my spiritual home.

Security around the embassy is incredible. Even though Turkey is a secular Muslim state, there are many fundamentalist Muslims here who are anti-Semitic. After going through a few checkpoints I'm told I have to make an appointment. I try to explain in English to an Israeli officer that I am a political asylum seeker who has crucial information about the thirteen Jews arrested in Iran, but he doesn't seem interested. 'Your appointment is for next Thursday,' he says.

Disappointed, we decide to save money by taking the bus back to the hotel. After standing for hours at a crowded stop in Taksim and saying 'Aksaray' to a few old Turkish women, we finally work out which is the right bus.

When we get off, Azita suggests wandering through the nearby bazaar before returning to the hotel, and as we walk I become aware of two Iranian-looking men behind us.

'Those two guys seem familiar,' I say to Azita.

She doesn't believe me until an hour later when, after changing direction many times, the two middle-aged men are still trailing us, pretending to shop. By now I'm certain they're from the intelligence service. I can sense those bastards.

'Yes, I remember them,' Azita says suddenly. 'They were on our bus when we left Iran. One of them walked past me in the restaurant before Tabriz and ordered lunch. You're right, they could be following us.'

I tell Azita and the girls to go to a different shop while I head in another direction and exit the bazaar through a plaza. An hour later I join them in the hotel lobby. We wait for forty minutes but there's no trace of the men. I feel a little easier, though I can't imagine we've lost them permanently, and I know from bitter experience what these people are capable of.

That night I lie in the darkness trying to push away the memories. They burst forth from malevolent times like fresh blood from an old wound.

It was a freezing afternoon in the winter of 1997. Over the last few months more than eighty writers and journalists who had criticised the Islamic regime had disappeared, their bodies later found in bags on roadsides. They had been kidnapped and slaughtered by MOIS officers.

I was walking home from work through a backstreet in Mashhad. Nobody else was around and the only sound was of a crow cawing on a leafless oak tree. Suddenly a car turned into the narrow street. I kept walking, hoping it would drive past me, even though not a lot of traffic came this way. I heard the car slow down behind me. I compelled myself to keep going but my knees felt like melting wax.

The car came to a halt and I heard two doors open. I saw in my peripheral vision two men stepping out and I could hear their footsteps heading towards me. I continued on, slowly. Soon they had caught up and were flanking me, one on each side.

'Mr Karimi? Kooshyar Karimi?' I stopped immediately. I knew what this meant. For at least five years, since I first saved the life of a desperate girl by repairing her hymen, I had been expecting the black car to appear.

'Yes?' I turned my head to the right and saw a bearded man in his thirties wearing a dark grey suit.

'Come with us,' he said. He and his colleague squeezed my arms firmly.

'What is this about?' I asked.

'Just a few questions,' said the man on my left, pulling my arm. Though resistance was useless, I struggled to free myself.

'I haven't done anything,' I said. What a stupid statement. Big Brother knew very well what I had done. Now he would crush me, like an elephant tramping on a fly.

'Get in the car,' demanded a third man, who had just joined the other two. All wore grey suits and plain white shirts, had well-trimmed black beards and very short hair. I was certain they had guns. I'd managed to stay hidden for such a long time, but that was now over. On this icy afternoon, in this silent narrow lane, I knew my life was about to end.

The heavily built men dragged me to the car, where there was another man waiting for us. I was quickly blindfolded and pushed under the back seat, with one man on each side of me. The man on my left was virtually resting his feet on my back. My face was close to the floor, my lips brushing against the carpet. I found it extremely hard to breathe.

The car travelled fast, stopping briefly only three times. We made several turns but it was impossible to guess which direction we were heading in. I imagined the car sweeping through the busy streets of Mashhad and thought the driver must be exceptionally skilled. During the long, agonising journey the men seldom spoke. The blindfold pressed hard against my eyes.

Another five minutes or so passed. The man in the front passenger seat said something to the driver but I couldn't make out his words.

'Ahmad, make sure you take it with you,' said the man on my left. *Ahmad. His name is Ahmad.* That was what I would tell a jury if I survived and managed to escape to a democratic country. I would tell them that four men from MOIS kidnapped and tortured me and finally, once they had extracted all I had to tell them, they stood me against a wall and shot me dead.

Eventually, the car began slowing down. When it stopped for a few seconds, I heard a gate opening outside and a guard saying something. We momentarily moved forward once more, until the engine was abruptly turned off. All the men got out. It was such a relief when the weight of the legs was lifted off me, but one of the men grabbed my arm again. 'Get out!' After struggling to emerge with my eyes covered, I managed to place a foot on the ground. I felt sunshine on my face and fresh air on my skin.

'Walk!' The man pulled me along, my arm in his powerful grip. I had no doubt he was leading me to a secret house, and what was likely to follow. I thought, I'm so sorry, Newsha. I've tried hard to protect you and provide you with everything, but I've failed. Please forgive me, my little princess. What would happen to her if I were jailed or executed?

I was thrown onto a small metal chair, my eyes still covered and my hands now tied behind me. Hours dragged by. I was not allowed to leave the chair. Every now and then I gently shifted my legs and arms, wiggling my toes and fingers, to make sure I was still alive.

Another three or four hours passed. I was sure it was now long past midnight. My family must have been contacting hospitals, the police, hotels and everybody they knew to find me. The intelligence service never gave information to prisoners' families, even several days following an arrest. If you were taken by MOIS, you simply disappeared.

Though I'd experienced violence at the hands of my father and school bullies, I knew that MOIS officers were masters at inflicting a fundamentally different form of pain. MOIS was a university of human suffering, its graduates expert torturers who did not think or feel and who were programmed to slaughter their victims.

After another hour or so, I couldn't hold my bladder anymore. It was like an overinflated ball about to explode.

'Help! Please!' I yelled. 'I need to go to the toilet!' No response. After another five minutes of twisting and turning, my limbs like frozen dough, I fell off the chair, which toppled over next to me. When I hit the ground I felt a warm liquid spread across my thighs and legs. I was extremely embarrassed; even as a child I'd hardly wet the bed. I tried to get up and grab the chair. I had to sit back on it before anyone noticed. But it was too late – I heard the door being flung open and footsteps coming rapidly towards me.

'Sorry, I was —' I began, but was stopped by a massive blow to my head. Lights flashed behind my eyes but before I registered any pain, another strike sent me back to the floor.

'You filthy motherfucking Jew. I told you to stay on that chair.' Punches and kicks rained all over my body. In a futile attempt to protect myself, I curled into a ball but was kicked hard in the face. Blood streamed down my cheeks and chin. The ache in my stomach was so severe I couldn't breathe for several seconds. This assault was worse than anything I'd ever experienced. All I could do was mumble, 'Please . . . stop . . . please . . .' And then I passed out.

When I opened my eyes again, I saw a blurry fluorescent light behind metal bars in the ceiling. I realised I was alone in a cell, and my hands were no longer tied. My wrists were swollen, I had an excruciating headache, and the slightest eye movement was agony. I wondered how long I had been there. Every breath was like a scalpel digging into my ribs.

I felt a rush of salty fluid in my throat. I tried to swallow it but, gagging at the taste, spat it out instead. It was blood. Although I was light-headed, my medical knowledge surfaced: I was sure I had a fracture at the base of my skull. Before long the concrete floor was strewn with bright red saliva. I hoped I didn't have bleeding in my brain.

I eventually stood up. My right thigh was severely bruised, and when I stretched I felt a sharp pain in my stomach and back. I nearly passed out again, but managed to hold on to the wall.

Before I could take a step I threw up. I can't give in, I told myself. I need to stay alive for Newsha.

But after several hours of intense pain and boredom, I felt pushed towards complying with whatever these bastards wanted. In the windowless, airless cell, the only sensory stimuli were the stench of puke and the fluorescent light behind its own metal bars. Alone and defenceless, I had no idea how long I would be kept there or if they were going to hang me.

Days passed. The heavy metal door was only opened for meals and prayers. In Islamic Iran everyone must pray at least three times a day, and I had to keep pretending I was a Muslim. They fed me bread, dates, rice and feta, and butter and jam, always served by the same tall, slim guard. I was given a long loose shirt and pants to wear but no shoes or belt, to prevent me from hanging myself. My wounds gradually began to heal, and I spent most of my time pacing up and down the cell. I struggled to sleep; when I eventually dozed off, I had dreadful nightmares.

On around the eighth day after my arrest I was sitting on the floor, thinking about Newsha, when the door opened and the same officer as usual entered. But this time I knew he had not come to give me my meal.

'Get up and turn around,' he ordered, and then blindfolded me tightly.

He grabbed my arm and led me down the corridor. I sensed other cells around us and heard a man screaming and begging. Horror engulfed my body and I could barely walk. The officer pulled me along, like a *haji* dragging his sacrificial lamb behind him before cutting its throat. At the end of the corridor we entered a room.

'Put him here,' said another male voice. Two heavy arms pushed me facedown onto something that felt like a metal bed. My wrists and ankles were tied to its corners.

'Please, I have a daughter . . . She is only three years old . . .' I pleaded, but before I could utter another word a thick cloth was crammed into my mouth.

'Shut up!' The cloth was pushed in further, stinking of old blood and vomit. I gagged and struggled to breathe. My shirt was ripped open, and my whole body tensed.

'One!' A snake's tooth dug into the naked flesh on my back.

'Two!' I was screaming through the cloth.

'Three!' As the lash cut deeper into my skin, I bit so hard into the cloth that its fibres began ripping in my mouth.

'Eleven, twelve, thirteen, fourteen . . .'

I no longer felt the blows. Under such torment, my body's natural coping mechanism had come to my rescue, and I began floating in a weightless trance.

'Promise me you'll become a doctor and help the people in the slums.' My mother's voice echoed in my ears. I was eight years old and in hospital, critically ill with typhoid. 'I've asked Adonai to save you, and in return you'll study medicine,' she said firmly. I knew how powerful my mother was, and Adonai too. Two years earlier, I'd been cowering in our basement during a storm when my mother told me I was one of the Children of Israel, whom Adonai had protected for thousands of years – and that he would protect me too. I no longer felt afraid, and instantly became a Jew in every crevice of my body and soul.

'Fifty-three, fifty-four . . .' my torturer continued, panting between each forceful stroke. I concentrated on my Adonai, and took comfort from the idea that I was sacrificing myself in the struggle for freedom.

The people who put me through this suffering were not inherently evil, but rather the products of the system in which they worked. I could forgive them – not because I was extraordinarily benevolent, or because I believed God would punish them, but because their brutality was an inevitable result of the country's religious autocracy. In Islamic Iran, intelligence agents believe absolutely in the sacredness of the regime and their role as punishers of infidels.

But these men were only experts in physical torture. My psychological torturer, Haji Samadi, was a high-ranking officer in MOIS. He did have a natural talent for stripping people of their values and identity and transforming them into silent machines that obeyed only him, doing whatever he decreed to avoid his wrath. He knew that torture is necessary to subordinate the intelligent, and fear is the best tool to create self-censorship. After a session with Samadi, his victim would do anything to avoid another one, even commit suicide. Samadi scarred my soul, forever.

THREE

The next morning I go to reception to call my family in Israel. Though it's expensive, we need their help. After five rings a child answers in Hebrew. 'Is your maman home?' I ask. 'I would like to speak to her.'

After a pause I hear a woman's voice. 'Ilana, is that you?' I ask.

Ilana is my mother's cousin and has been living in Israel since the revolution, when more than seventy-five percent of Iranian Jews fled the country.

When I tell her who I am, she starts crying. 'Kooshyar! Uncle Abraham's nephew! Where are you?' I explain my situation briefly.

'Listen to me, Kooshyar. Don't worry. Go to your appointment at the Israeli embassy and tell them what you've told me. They'll help you get here and as soon as you arrive I'll pick you up from Ben Gurion Airport. We will help you settle in Israel. You'll be safe, I promise.'

Ilana's words are heaven-sent and I immediately feel relieved for the first time since leaving Iran.

After thanking Ilana profusely, I go back to our room to tell everyone the good news. Ilana's family is very well established in Tel Aviv. All we have to do is wait a few days to get our visas.

At noon we go to a restaurant. I haven't felt this happy for a long time. Azita is concerned about the expense, but my appetite's returned and I want to celebrate our imminent journey. We order food and beer. Newsha keeps asking where her Nan and Pop and cousins are. I tell her we're going to a beautiful country and they'll join us soon.

Back in our hotel room, when Newsha and Niloofar are finally asleep, Azita says she wants to talk to me.

'Kooshyar, I have to be honest with you. I don't want to go to Israel. You know I don't want to raise my kids as Jews.'

'But that's fine, they can choose their own religion.'

'No, I've decided I'm not going. That's it.'

'But this is our only chance,' I plead. 'We can't stay here. They'll track me down. Plus we haven't got much money.'

She shakes her head.

'Listen to me, Azita, please! We've come this far. Let's just get to Israel, then if you're not happy after a couple of years we can move somewhere else.'

'If you want to go to Israel, go. I will take the kids back to Iran.'

I look at this woman – my wife, the mother of my daughters – and can hardly believe what she's telling me. Yet from the time

I was forced to marry her instead of Mahshid, whom I truly loved, I've seen how stubborn and narrow-minded Azita can be. She hates Jewish people. She knew when our marriage was arranged I had a Jewish background, but she thought I was a Muslim. When she found out that I'm Jewish through and through, she was outraged. We never should have married. It was only forty-eight hours between us meeting for the first time and the ceremony, so we didn't realise we hardly had a thought in common. Though I agreed to stop smoking, I sneak around finding places to light up; I also listen to Pink Floyd, whom she hates, in secret. I've attempted without the least success to get her interested in literature and philosophy.

I don't understand why Azita's anti-Semitic attitude is more important to her than our family's safety. What should I do? Azita is not in real danger, as she has an Iranian passport and in theory can return anytime. I could go to Tel Aviv with Newsha and Niloofar while Azita returned to Iran but the girls travel on her passport, and of course there's no way I can transfer them onto my fake one. Besides, Azita wouldn't agree to being separated from her children. But neither will I: the idea of living without my daughters appals me.

In the end, I surrender to my wife. After all, she has shared my exile until now and this has not been easy for her. However, I also know that it's unlikely Azita will return home. She has no education and no means of earning a living. She has to stay with me: divorce is unthinkably difficult and humiliating for Iranian women (that right belongs almost exclusively to men). Knowing this, I can't abandon her. 'Okay,' I say. 'We'll try other embassies tomorrow. Hopefully one of them will give us visas.'

Azita goes to sleep and I head to the balcony to have a cigarette. I look down at the lights and cars in the busy streets while I smoke – all those people going about their lives, having somewhere to call home. Beside me a moth flutters against a light bulb protruding from a rusted fitting on the wall, returning again and again in a futile attempt to find solace in the dim glow. I stub out my cigarette on the railing and watch the ash float down to the street. I feel as if my heart is on fire.

Next morning we set off for the American embassy. It's extremely hot and humid again and Niloofar is restless.

'Americans are big supporters of Jews. They'll help us,' I say to Azita as we get on the bus.

When we arrive there's a queue almost two kilometres long outside the huge building. All ages and races are here but most are from the Middle East. I ask several people what's happening, trying both Farsi and English, and am told they're lodging application forms for visitor and immigration visas. A Turkish man sitting behind a metal desk in the shade is selling the forms for one hundred dollars each, but fortunately I only need one for the four of us. After I've filled out all seven pages, we line up for five hours. Niloofar's nappy has to be changed three times.

Everyone in the queue is complaining about the embassy. 'Bastard Americans,' hisses a fat Lebanese man next to me. 'This is my second time applying. They won't give me a visa because they're racist.'

'This is our fifth try,' says the young woman in front of us. 'They'll probably never give us visitor visas, just because we're from Turkey.'

'Do you think we have any chance?' I ask her. 'We're from Iran.'

She smiles wryly. 'Isn't Iran one of America's biggest enemies? I don't think your chances are high, especially if you're applying for the whole family.' Her English is better than mine. Even though their governments have a close relationship, it seems that the Turks themselves aren't treated with much friendliness by the Americans. Despite what I've heard, I still cling to my belief we'll get visas because I'm a Jew. My Jewish blood brought me here – maybe it will save me.

It's late afternoon when we finally reach the front of the queue at the gate, where an official demands we hand over the form along with our documents. I'm surprised we're not even going to be dealt with inside the embassy.

He shakes his head as he looks through our form. 'You're from Iran.'

I whisper, 'Officer, please, I'm Jewish. We had to flee Iran because of the recent political unrest.'

'You're Jewish? Then come back tomorrow, but not here. You must go to the gate on the eastern side of the building, where there is a small door. Be there at two in the afternoon and someone will take care of you.'

When we return to the hotel I feel exhausted but full of hope. Azita, on the other hand, is sceptical. I look at Newsha, who was so tired when we got back she went straight to bed. Just a few days ago she had a big bedroom with a TV, VCR, lots of Disney movies and lovely dolls. Countless relatives would come by and pamper her. Now we are alone with nobody to support us.

The next day we go to the American embassy again. Even though it takes us some time to find the small door, we're early and have to wait an hour. When the door opens I tell the American official that I'm an Iranian Jew and was involved in the arrest of the thirteen Jews.

He nods. 'Show me your documentation. Your ID and your family's ID.'

I desperately search my bag. I have my Iranian driver's licence, some of my books, and Azita's passport. I show them to him but he's not convinced.

'I need to see proof that you're Jewish,' he says.

'I'm sorry, sir, but I had to escape. I didn't get a chance to collect many documents. I have ID for my wife.'

'No, I need to see yours.'

'Look at these books – my name is on the covers. Also, if you check your database you'll find me. I'm from the Haiim family. They've lived in Iran for fifty generations.'

'I'm sorry, I can't help you,' he says, before closing the door. We're devastated. We've spent more than a hundred and fifty dollars in the last two days trying to go to America. I knock on the door but I know it's pointless.

We go back to the hotel. The receptionist asks, 'How are things, my Iranian brother?'

'Fine, brother, fine,' I respond. I can't bear to tell him the truth.

There's a young Iranian couple at the desk and the woman is crying. 'They were following us and when we left the last shop one of them attacked me, grabbed my handbag and ran away. We reported it to the police but they're not doing anything. I've lost all my money and my passport. I don't know what to do.' She sobs and her husband shakes his head in frustration.

The receptionist shows little sympathy. 'The police are on the criminals' side because they get a kickback. I told you to be careful of your belongings.'

Walking upstairs, I touch the small bag holding all our documents and money. It's strapped to my waist but I realise that doesn't mean it's safe, as thieves here use Stanley knives to cut the straps of bags. If mine is stolen, the four of us will be on the streets.

We're all drained and exasperated when we reach our room. Newsha wants me to take her to the shops and I promise her we'll go tomorrow and I'll buy her a nice toy. She's still asking about her cousins, and I keep promising that we'll see them again very soon.

When the girls are asleep I go downstairs to buy another bottle of water. The receptionist watches me search for the right money in the bag strapped to my waist.

'Don't worry, brother.' He hands me a bottle of water, free of charge.

Over the next two days we visit various European embassies, from Britain and France to Cyprus and Albania. All of them say there are no visas for Iranian citizens, or that we don't have the correct documents, or that it will take about two years to process our application. We don't try the Australian embassy, as we've heard from other asylum seekers that Australia has a strict immigration policy and that it's impossible to get a visa.

Every afternoon on coming back, frustrated and shattered, to the hotel I see some Middle Eastern and Turkish men talking in the lobby. After sending Azita and the girls to our room I sit down and eavesdrop on their conversations. I soon realise that these men are called *insan kacakci*, which means people smugglers in Turkish. An Iranian couple staying in the hotel tell me that these are the people who can get you a fake passport and fly you to another country. For enough money you can go virtually anywhere.

'What happens when you arrive?' I ask them.

'Then you apply for asylum in that country and the authorities take care of you,' the young wife tells me.

'How much does it cost?'

'It depends on where you want to go and how many of you there are,' the husband responds. 'Everyone has a different fee but it seems to cost around ten thousand American dollars to go somewhere decent.'

I feel so disappointed. 'I only have three thousand at the most.'

'Well, maybe you could go to Greece, and then you might be able to try for a better country later on,' the young woman says.

I thank them and go back to our room, but I can't sleep. As I've done almost every night since we arrived, I stay awake and smoke Demir Teppe cigarettes, the cheapest and strongest in Istanbul.

On day seven someone in the Swiss embassy tells us about HIAS, an organisation that helps asylum seekers in immediate danger. I have a glimpse of hope again. The next day, after taking several buses and walking for ages, we finally find the right building. Before we go in I put my right hand on my heart and pray to my Adonai.

A middle-aged German woman in the office tells us that the organisation has helped thousands of religious minorities in the Middle East settle in other countries. She seems kind and I feel confident that my story will convince her to help us. While I'm excitedly explaining to her how I managed to escape from Iran, she interrupts me politely. 'Did you say you're a Jew?'

'Yes,' I say proudly.

A tight smile appears on her face, an expression I've seen often in the last eight days. 'I'm afraid we only help Catholic refugees,' she says, ending our conversation.

We return to the hotel, our hopes dashed yet again. I'm starting to panic. Our money won't last more than a few more weeks here. I knew that Iranians are almost never given visas but I really believed being a Jew would help.

It's nine o'clock and we're all tired out. Azita and the children go to sleep but I can't relax. I'm chain-smoking my horrible Turkish cigarettes when I decide to find a people smuggler. I know I probably don't have enough money, but it's worth a try.

I go down to the crowded lobby. On one side is a bar with a few people, mostly Iranians, dancing to loud music. An overdressed middle-aged man is sitting on a large lounge with a suitcase on his lap. I've seen him before and there's a good chance he's a people smuggler, so I go over to the couch and tell him I need some advice. Straight away he asks, 'You want to fly?'

'Excuse me?' I'm not sure what's distracting me more: the man's strange barcode-like fringe, or his funny tie that has exactly the same pattern as the tablecloth my mother used to place over her ancient black and white TV. When it stopped working four years ago, she turned the TV into a fish tank.

'I'm guessing you want to go overseas. Is that right?'

'Yes.' I'm suddenly brought back to the present, and am worried this man might work for Iranian Intelligence.

'I think I've seen you with a young woman and two kids.'

'That's right.'

'Where would you like to go?'

'To be honest I'd go anywhere, but Canada or the USA would be great.'

'No problem, brother. I can get all of you there in three days.'

'Are you sure?'

'Of course. This is my job.' I should've come to this guy instead of wasting time and money on different embassies. I sit down next to him.

'How much will it cost?'

'Four people to the USA is twelve thousand dollars, and for Canada it's ten thousand.' When he sees the look on my face he says, 'Believe me, brother, I'm giving you a discount because you have little children. The real price is normally around sixteen and twelve.'

'No, this is too much. I can't afford it.'

'People smuggling is expensive, brother – you can ask around but be careful. A lot of these guys are crooks. They'll take your money and disappear. But not me. I take half now and half when you arrive.'

'How does it work?'

'I'll buy foreign passports for all of you – I know people who steal them from tourists, but they cost a lot – and put your pictures in them. Then we get plane tickets for the country the passports are from. Sometimes we have to disguise you a bit, by bleaching your hair or using makeup. If you can't afford American or Canadian passports, ones from the Netherlands are cheaper – seven grand – and you can go to Canada as Dutch citizens. All you'll need to do is talk gibberish to the customs officers as nobody knows Dutch.'

'Thanks for your help, but I don't have seven grand either.'

'Okay, brother. Good luck, but I don't think you'll get anywhere without that sort of money.'

Just after I've got up from the couch, a man with a big belly approaches me. 'Iranian?' he asks in a harsh voice.

'Yes.'

'Wanna fly?' He gestures with his hand.

'Yes, in fact.'

'Follow me.' He walks over to a chair in another corner. 'I can fly you to Germany or the Netherlands for eight thousand dollars.'

'I'm sorry, I don't have that much. Can you please do it for less? We're desperate. If I go back to Iran they will hang me. Please, sir, for God's sake, help me.'

He sighs. 'I understand, brother, but passports and tickets are expensive.' He has a thick Turkish accent. 'I think I can do it for six thousand eight hundred, but that's my lowest price.'

This is a crushing blow. I decide not to beg anymore, but as I'm going back to the room a sturdy bald man in a black jacket grabs my arm. 'Come with me, brother,' he says. He has a big scar on his left cheek and a heavy gold chain around his wide neck. His top shirt buttons are undone, revealing thick black hair on his chest. I sit down next to him on a couch.

'Iranian? And you want go USA?' His English is much worse than the last man's.

'I would go anywhere. I promise I'll take any job there and send money back to you. I was a doctor in Iran.'

'If you were doctor, you are loaded.'

'No, things are . . . complicated. I lost everything because I had to flee overnight. I'm not lying, brother – please believe me. I need to protect my children.'

'How much you have?'

'Only three thousand dollars.'

The sturdy man scratches his head. 'I take you Greece with that money.'

I want to hug him. 'Really?'

'Yes. I fly many refugees. How old your kids?'

'One is five and the other is two months old.'

'God bless! I have seven kids.' He shows six fingers with his hands. 'The oldest is twenty-four. Youngest is half past two.' Then he gets down to business. 'We have to go ten hours by boat and then eight hours walk in jungle. Can you carry your kids?'

'Of course I can.'

'I will come with you to jungle and then I show you way and you will go Greece. Near Greece, police will stop you. Tell them you are asylum seeker and they take you detention centre. It's safe and has food and everything. And they send you to a nice Europe country in three months.'

This is wonderful news. 'Thank you so much, brother. God bless you.'

'I organise things in two days, but I need money. I bribe some people for this, you have to give me two thousand tomorrow and rest when we depart.'

'No problem, brother.'

'Okay.' Then he lowers his voice. 'Do not talk to anybody about this, understand?'

'Of course.'

'I see you here tomorrow night at nine.' And off he goes.

I'm so full of joy that I decide to have a beer at the bar and enjoy the music. A few minutes later a young man leaves the dance floor and sits down next to me. He starts talking in Farsi.

'What are you doing here?' I ask.

'Just having fun. That girl really likes me, I might get lucky tonight.' Then he adds, 'Are you staying in this shithole?'

'Yes, with my family.'

'Be very careful. There are a lot of crooks and violent people in this area. They'll rob and even stab you, especially after dark.'

'I'm from the slums, so I'm familiar with violence.'

'No, brother, this is not Iran. They can do anything to you – the police here are corrupt. Make sure you put your money in the bank. Never carry it with you.'

'How do I open an account?'

'It's very simple. Go to Iş Bank, show some ID and they'll open an account for you. You can access it whenever from anywhere in Turkey. But don't change your money into Turkish lira because its value drops all the time. Leave it as US dollars and each morning withdraw just enough for the day.'

'Thank you so much for your help.'

'I'm Saeed, by the way, from Tehran.'

I shake Saeed's hand. 'Karim.' I don't want to reveal my identity. I leave the bar and am walking towards the stairs when the receptionist calls me over to him.

He leans forward and speaks quietly. 'I noticed you talking to the smugglers.'

'Yes.'

'Listen, most of these guys are criminals, especially the last one you spoke to. His name's Mustafa and he's an armed robber on the run. He's very dangerous.'

'But he promised to take me and my family to Greece.'

The receptionist grins. 'He doesn't know which way is Greece. All he wants to know is how much money you have.' Then he looks at me intently. 'You didn't tell him you have money, did you?'

I admit I did and he shakes his head. 'How silly. He might

even come to your room tonight and turn his gun on you. Just make sure you lock your door and don't open it for anyone. Never talk to him again.'

I thank the receptionist for his advice and go back to the room, downcast and now also scared for my children's safety. I lock the door and hardly sleep all night.

FOUR

I'd been in prison for about three weeks, maybe longer. On this day I was taken to a different room and placed on a metal chair, my eyes covered and my hands tied behind my back. I had no idea what was about to happen, but was sure it would involve further torture.

A man came into the room, told me his name was Samadi and stood next to my chair. 'How are you, Dr Karimi?' he asked sarcastically. I told him I was fine. I wondered if he was going to hit me.

He said, 'I'm going to give you a pen and paper and leave the room. While I'm gone, I want you to write down the names of all the Zionists you've ever been in contact with, and the names of all the women whose pregnancies you've terminated and the girls whose virginities you've repaired. You must also tell me about the book you've been writing.'

'What book?' I asked. A hard blow almost sent me off the chair. The left side of my face was numb with pain and flashing lights appeared behind my eyes again.

'We know everything,' he said. His face was so close to mine I could smell onion on his breath. 'You can't hide anything from us. Write those names on that piece of paper. You have half an hour.' He untied my hands and left the room.

I removed the blindfold, grabbed the pen and started writing. I explained that I did believe in Islam, that my father was a Muslim, that I'd never terminated a pregnancy or restored anyone's virginity. I wrote that I had no Zionist friends and no sympathy for Israel or Jews, that I respected the Islamic government and was obedient to the Supreme Leader. I knew it was unlikely they'd believe me.

Before Samadi re-entered the room he ordered me to put the blindfold back on. I could see his black boots as I heard him pick up the paper.

'What is this bullshit?' He threw it at my face. 'When we searched your house, we found the Torah and pictures of Moses. You've written hundreds of pages about Jews. Are you denying all this?' His foul breath made me gag. 'Do you remember Mrs Razavi? You terminated her pregnancy. Are you telling me this didn't happen?'

I was shocked. I'd treated Mrs Razavi almost two years before. She had become pregnant after committing adultery with a man she loved.

'Don't worry, I'm going to make you talk.' Samadi turned on his heel and slammed the door.

This time they left me alone for several painful days. My mind drifted over events from the past, events that had led to this moment, such as when I sat my final high school exam.

Almost three hundred thousand students also took the exam that day, all over the country. The Iran–Iraq war was at its height and about one and a half million people had died. Saddam Hussein had started using chemical weapons against the Iranian forces and both countries were firing missiles into each other's major cities. I was eighteen and knew that if I failed, I would go straight to compulsory military service and that after forty-five days' basic training I would be at the front line, where I would probably be killed in less than three months.

The exam lasted eight hours with only a thirty-minute break. I'd memorised all the formulae, all the information I thought I'd need for biology, chemistry, physics, literature, religion, history, sociology, mathematics, algebra, geometry and geology. I'd studied as hard as possible, knowing I had to get at least ninety-seven percent to qualify for medical school, fulfilling my promise to my mother. When it was over, though, I was despondent: I was sure I'd failed.

I had to wait five weeks for the results to arrive in the mail. My mother prayed, and Koorosh was nearly as nervous as I was. On the day the letter arrived, Koorosh collected it and handed it to me without a word.

I stared at the envelope for a few moments, took a deep breath and lifted the flap. Inside was a small slip of paper with computer-generated numbers and letters on it. I scanned through the list of subjects with my results next to them, and saw my total result at the bottom. I had to read it several times, unable to believe my eyes.

'Ninety-nine point two percent. I'm ranked eighty-seventh in the entire country!' I was absolutely exhilarated. A second later Koorosh, my mother and I were jumping and dancing around the room.

With my excellent results, I was eligible to go to any university in Iran. I chose the medical school in Mashhad and sent off the application forms. A month later, when the university entrance results were due to be published, I rushed to the newspaper kiosk early in the morning. Hundreds of students were already waiting there.

When the truck finally delivered the newspapers I fought my way through the crowd, managed to grab a copy and began searching feverishly. I saw pictures of the top ten students in the country, but mine was not there. I started checking eleven pages of numbers and university places. I couldn't find my name.

I walked home numb and full of shame. My mother and Koorosh also looked through the paper several times but without success. Then Koorosh saw an official notice: *The people whose names are not printed in this newspaper have been rejected by the Islamic Investigation Committee because they have not qualified as pious Muslims deserving to be accepted into a university. Nevertheless they can send a letter of appeal to the Committee and have their case reviewed if they believe that they have strong reason to do so.*

We were in shock. Koorosh and I'd thought we were doing a great job of pretending to be Muslims. My closest friend, Masood, who had grown up with me and gone to the same school, never had the slightest clue I was anything but a devout Muslim. This was the first time I realised I couldn't keep any secrets from MOIS. I hadn't been able to convince the ayatollacracy that I was a loyal dog.

I wanted to leave, to escape this vile regime. I spoke to Jewish relatives in Isfahan who promised to get me a fake passport, so I could go to Turkey and from there to Israel.

For three nights I couldn't sleep, planning my escape. And then on the fourth day my friend Majid Vahidi came to visit me. I'd been tutoring him in maths, physics and chemistry, and my mother was his family's cleaner for two years. Majid's father was one of the top respiratory physicians in Iran, a graduate of a reputable American university, the dean of the medical school and the principal of Imam Reza Hospital, a vast modern teaching hospital. He was also a member of Imam Khomeini's medical team.

Majid said that when he told his father about my rejection from university, Dr Vahidi was furious and had insisted I appeal, putting his name as a referee. According to Majid he said, 'They will then contact me and I'll fix it using my connections. If there's one student who deserves to go to medical school in this country, it's Kooshyar.'

I sent the appeal letter. After an agonising four-month wait, during which there was no news from my Jewish relatives, Dr Vahidi asked my mother and me to come to his house one afternoon. We went to their mansion, which was full of luxury furniture and expensive paintings.

Dr Vahidi said, 'Two Revolutionary Guards came to see me today. They were asking about you, Kooshyar.' He looked at me seriously. 'I told them you're a very pious Muslim who prays three times a day on time, that you fast at Ramadan and are faithful to the Islamic government.'

Dr Vahidi was well aware none of this was true.

'I agreed to sign a guarantor form to allow you to go to the university, but you have to behave or I will be in trouble. Do you understand, Kooshyar?'

'Yes, sir. Thank you so much . . .' His generosity overwhelmed me.

'I'm from a poor family too, and I know how hard it is to make it to this level. I helped you because I truly believe you deserve to go to university, and I'm sure you'll become a wonderful doctor.'

I had tears in my eyes. My mother went to Dr Vahidi's chair. 'Dr Vahidi, you are an angel sent by God to save my son's life.' And she bowed to him.

When we left the house Dr Vahidi said to me, 'Go and celebrate tonight with your family, Dr Karimi!'

I wish I could've kept my vow not to upset the Islamic regime in any way. But when a 22-year-old woman told me she'd attempted suicide because her secret boyfriend had made her pregnant and refused to marry her, I agreed to terminate her pregnancy. I did it to save her life. I couldn't refuse her cry for help, nor the cries of many other women. And so I became an abortionist.

On the sixtieth day after my arrest, Samadi came back and interrogated me for four hours. At the end, he gave me one option to avoid execution: 'You work for us.' I had absolutely no choice.

Two days later I was released, and my life as a traitor began.

The next morning I tell Azita about the people smugglers. She says that under no circumstances would she go with them. It's too dangerous.

We go to Iş Bank and I open an account with my driver's licence. The teller treats me like a king. Because Turkey's in an economic crisis, its banks are grateful for deposits of any amount.

Not knowing what else to do, we get on a bus and go to the Indonesian embassy. We spend four hours there just to be told we can't get a visa unless it's for a short visit. Another waste of time and money on bus fare.

We return to the hotel disheartened. In the lobby I meet Saeed again and he invites me for a drink. I tell him about the conversation with the people smugglers.

'Stay away from them, Karim,' he warns me. I feel bad giving him a false name when he's been so kind to me, but I have to be careful around Iranians.

'I have to get my family somewhere safe.'

'Turkey isn't safe for you at all. Iran exchanges Kurdistan Workers' Party members for Iranian dissidents who've fled to Turkey. A lot of Iranians disappear here.'

Suddenly he becomes excited. 'You must go to the United Nations in Ankara, to the UNHCR. My cousin went there and they supported him and sent him to Germany four years ago.'

'Really?'

'Yes. The UN helps people like you. You're basically a refugee. But you only have ten days from your arrival to go to their office; otherwise, it becomes more difficult to apply. You have to wait at least a year for an interview and in the meantime they make you regularly exit and re-enter the country. How long have you been here so far?'

'Nine days.'

'Karim, you must go now! There are buses to Ankara till midnight. If you make the last one, you'll be there in the morning and can go to the UN office straight away.'

I look at the time: nine o'clock. I put down my beer and start running towards our room, but turn around when Saeed yells, 'The UN is "Birlashmish Milatlar" in Turkish.' It's the last time I see him. He's been a true friend.

When I rush into the room, Azita has just got Niloofar to sleep. 'We need to pack, Azita. We're going to Ankara.'

With Newsha asleep in my arms, I pay for our stay while Azita tries to calm down Niloofar, who's woken up screaming in panic. The hotel cost three hundred and sixty dollars for nine nights. As we leave I bump into Mustafa in the doorway.

'Hello, brother,' he says. 'Ready to go?'

'We're actually going to a friend's house for the night. I'll be back tomorrow and we can discuss more details about our deal then.'

Mustafa looks at the four of us. 'You go to friend this time of night?' He checks his watch.

'Yes, I just realised one of my friends from Iran is in Istanbul and he's willing to lend me some money. I need to see him tonight.' I move past him.

'I see you tomorrow here, hey?' he yells as we hurry away.

We catch a taxi to the bus terminal, a vast dark area. I walk as fast as I can to the ticket counters of each bus company but most of them are closed. I ask the ones that are open, 'Ankara?' and people keep shaking their heads. After fifteen minutes I realise we're too late. I'm distraught. We can't go back to the hotel – we've spent a lot of money to get here. The thought of sleeping in the street overnight and being too late for the UN is making me panic. Then at the far end of the terminal I see two offices with lights still on.

'Come on, Azita!' I start running, Azita and the girls trailing behind me. I go into the first office. 'Ankara?'

'Konya,' says the Turkish man behind the desk.

'Ankara, please!'

The Turkish man says something and points at the office next door. I race over. 'Ankara? Please?'

A young man is yawning at his desk. 'Kach keshi?' he says.

'Ankara!' I repeat.

He looks at Azita, who's just stepped into the office, and raising his index finger says, 'Sadejeh birkeshi.' I realise he's trying to tell us there's only one ticket left.

'Okay,' I say. But he shakes his head, counting us. I indicate that Azita and I will hold the girls on our laps and I'll sit on the floor. He shakes his head again, gets up and starts turning out the lights.

'Please, abi,' Azita begs. The Turkish man looks at Niloofar crying in Azita's arms and hesitates.

'Okay.' He sits back on his chair. 'A hundred and forty-five dollars.' I know this is four times the normal price but I hand over the money. We run to platform 12, at the other end of the terminal, carrying the children. The bus is full but it's there, waiting for us, it seems. When we get on, the driver glares and mutters the same word the passengers on the bus to Istanbul called us: *evsiz*. I later learn this means 'homeless savages'.

We find the last empty seat, which is at the back of the bus. Azita sits in it with Niloofar in her arms and I settle on the floor between two rows of seats, holding Newsha. The Turkish passengers look at us and whisper.

At ten minutes past midnight the bus starts moving. Just like on the bus to Istanbul, when Azita changes Niloofar's nappy several passengers complain loudly about the smell, and even the bus driver yells out something I don't comprehend.

Eventually everyone falls asleep, except for the driver, Azita and me. 'What does "abi" mean?' I ask her.

'"Brother". I learned it in Istanbul from an Iranian woman,' she says. We smile at each other for the first time in nine days.

The trip takes the whole night. We go through a series of mountains and plains, but it's too dark to enjoy the scenery. At four in the morning the bus stops at a café. Most Turks are Sunni Muslims, who pray five times a day, so the passengers get off for a quick tea and prayer. Azita and I leave the bus for some fresh air. A young Turkish family passes by with a little girl who's licking a candy. Newsha stares at her.

'Would you like a candy, sweetheart?' I ask her.

She just shakes her head.

'Why not? I know you love candies.'

'No, Baba jan, they're expensive,' she says. Her words shock me. I'm appalled she even knows what 'expensive' means. 'I know we don't have money and we shouldn't buy candies or toys,' she tells me.

'Who told you that?'

'You said to Maman yesterday not to buy that shirt and those expensive nappies because if our money runs out we'll be poor.'

This makes me feel terrible. I realise how intelligent and sensitive children are.

'Newsha, I was just kidding. Husbands sometimes say these things to their wives, and wives sometimes say them to their husbands, just to stop wasting money.' I tell her we'll soon be going to Disneyland, and buy a candy for her. It costs one dollar, more than a loaf of bread, but I want my daughter to feel safe and happy.

At seven-thirty the bus arrives in Ankara. Azita and I are exhausted. Though we know the driver will rip us off because we're foreigners, we take a taxi to 'Birlashmish Milatlar'. After half an hour, we stop in a small street.

About forty people of all ages and skin colours are standing in front of a building with a United Nations sign on it, and more people join the crowd every minute. A man in his mid-forties walks over to the group and sits on the ground. A wave of noise erupts around him and when I go closer I see that he's stitched his lips together. A woman and four small children are sitting near him, and I keep Newsha away. Azita finds a young Iranian couple and starts conversing with them. The man's name is Arya and his wife is Shadi. They've been living here for a month already and know a few Turkish words.

'The UN is hopeless,' he tells us, shaking his head. 'When you first go in, they make a file and give you a time for an interview, which you have to come back for. In the interview, you have to prove you'll be executed for non-criminal reasons if you go back to Iran. If they do recognise you as a refugee and send you to a third country, you don't get to choose which one.'

'How long does the whole process take?' I ask Arya.

'More than a year at best, usually two or three years. As soon as you go inside they give you brochures with the latest statistics on asylum seekers. According to those more than ninety-five percent of cases are rejected.' My heart sinks.

'What if you can't convince them you're a refugee?' Azita asks.

'You can appeal,' Shadi says, 'but it takes more than three years to have your case reopened and get another interview.' She points at the man with stitched lips. 'That's what's happened to him. Poor man has been here seven years with his four kids. He's a Kurd from the west part of Iran.'

'You should never do anything like that,' Arya insists. 'If you try any form of protest, you'll be arrested and they'll close your file forever. If you do anything wrong, even steal a loaf of bread, you'll be deported.'

'They're brutal,' Shadi says.

'So why has he done this?' Azita asks.

'He's had enough. He told us the other day he'd prefer to be sent back to Iran and hanged.'

'How do you survive for such a long time here while you're waiting to be processed?' I ask Arya.

'You must have money with you because as an asylum seeker you're not allowed to have a job. If you work and the police find out you'll be deported.'

'Does the UN give you money?'

Arya laughs. 'Are you kidding? We're nothing to them. The UN only protects you if your interview is successful and you're recognised as a legitimate refugee.'

I steer Azita away. 'We can't do this. We don't have enough money to survive for more than a year here, even if our case is accepted.'

'But we've no other option. We have to try, Kooshyar.'

'No, I'm going to Israel.'

'Then I'll take the kids with me to Iran. *We* can still live there – it's you who has the problem.'

Two police cars turn up, and several officers try to drag the man with stitched lips into one of the cars. He resists, and his kids start crying. His wife screams and a policeman hits her. I cover Newsha's eyes. Finally it all ends and the whole family are taken away. Everyone watching is shaken.

'Now he'll be deported,' says Arya sadly. My heart aches. I have no hope or faith in the UN.

An hour passes and a young man appears, wearing an expensive suit with a thick gold chain around his neck. He's Turkish but speaks English very well, and he hands out some business cards.

'I work for Mr Kamal, an excellent Turkish lawyer. He used to be at the UN so he knows all the tricks to prepare your case. He'll give you a story guaranteed to be accepted, and his fees are quite reasonable.' I grab a card but a minute later a young Iranian man comes up to me.

'Don't go to that bastard. He's a charlatan. I paid him five hundred dollars and he gave me the same story he gives to everyone. My case was immediately rejected.'

I thank him and throw the card away. I look up in frustration and notice a few men on the balcony of one of the surrounding buildings looking at us. One man is taking photos.

'Iranian agents might be watching us,' I whisper to Azita.

At nine o'clock, two security guards open the gate and the crowd rushes forward. 'Line up and stay calm,' the guards order.

They let people in one by one. After three hours Azita, the girls and I reach the front of the queue. Newsha is hungry and keeps falling asleep in my arms. We're guided to a small office where a young man is sitting behind a desk.

'Show me your ID,' he says without eye contact. At least he speaks English.

He looks through Azita's passport. 'What about you?' he asks me.

'I had to flee from Iran, so I only have my driver's licence.'

'Give me that,' he demands. After photocopying the documents, he orders us to stand against the wall so he can take a photo. 'Hold the girls up a bit higher. Yes, that's fine.' Then he tells us to wait and disappears into another room.

A few minutes later he comes out holding a piece of paper with English and Turkish words on it and two pictures of us.

'This is your ID in Turkey from now on. Your appointment is in three months, on 12 September, and the UN is not responsible for you until your case is accepted. Now you must go register with the Turkish police as asylum seekers and surrender your passport and any other identification.' Then he walks away.

'This is ridiculous,' I tell Azita as the guard directs us out of the building. 'We can't survive here for another three months and then wait however long to get the results. We must go to Israel.'

'No, Kooshyar.' Azita storms off. 'It's all your fault we're now here like a bunch of homeless beggars. Look at us!' She starts crying, as do Niloofar and Newsha.

'Okay, I'm sorry.' I walk behind Azita, trying to calm her down. 'Let's go find a place to stay for the night.'

Though Ankara is much cheaper than Istanbul, I don't know how we'll survive more than a few months in Turkey.

FIVE

I was kidnapped for the second time in May 1997. This time they took me to an abandoned garage outside Mashhad and handcuffed me to a metal chair. I was surrounded by four men and was shocked to see that one of them was Mr Sayar, an old photographer MOIS had sent me to spy on. My job had been to become his friend and get the many photos he'd taken of Jews. After a few meetings Sayar gave me several photos showing Jewish people at their festivals or celebrations. Not wanting to condemn innocent people, I came to the foolish conclusion that if I proved I was not a good spy they might let me go. So I passed on to Samadi only half of the pictures Sayar had given me. I now realised sending me to him was a test of my obedience.

Sayar stood in front of me, grinning bitterly. Two sturdy young men held my arms firmly while Sayar lit a cigarette and walked slowly towards me.

'I told you to be careful, Kooshyar, didn't I?' His legs were touching my knees. 'I'm going to teach you a lesson today, a painful lesson.' He dragged on his cigarette and flicked the ash off the tip. He then put his knee on my chest, creating a crushing pressure, and burned my skin with the lighted end of his cigarette.

'You Jews are cancer cells. You're the AIDS virus,' he said through clenched teeth.

I wished I knew a different way of responding to the pain, because screaming and twisting my limbs seemed ridiculously inadequate. The man on my right punched me in the face to shut me up, but it didn't work. At least being punched distracted me from the burning sensation on my chest. I was afraid they'd crack my head again. After the last incarceration I spent almost a month in hospital with a fractured skull, leaving me with debilitating headaches. I knew that if it happened again I would die.

After taking another drag Sayar put his cigarette against the left side of my bare chest, then the right.

'Let go,' he barked at the other men, like a hunter dismissing his dogs. 'Undo his handcuffs.'

One of the men cut the plastic band around my wrists with a Stanley knife. He was clearly reluctant to do so but Sayar knew that what he'd done had left me a broken man. The word 'Islam' means 'surrender' or 'submission'. What a perfect name, I thought.

'I'll do whatever you want,' I managed to say to Sayar. I was his. I no longer existed. I would've been happy to die at any moment but

I could not tolerate one more minute of this agony.

Sayar smiled.

We catch a minibus to Ankara's police headquarters, a giant complex with a seemingly endless number of departments. The more
oppressive the regime, the more intricate its law enforcement. We
finally find the large hall for asylum seekers and there are many
people already there – including a lot of Iranians – waiting to be
processed. I see three officers arresting a group of young Russian
women for illegally working as prostitutes.

It's now eleven-thirty and Newsha is starving, so I go back
outside and purchase a small sandwich for her from a mobile cart.
After waiting three hours in the hall, we're finally called into the
chief superintendent's room. He's around fifty, and makes it clear
he's tired of dealing with illegal immigrants and asylum seekers. He
looks at the paper with our photos on it, given to us by the UN.

'Iranian?' he asks without looking at us.

'Yes, sir,' I reply.

'What are you doing in Turkey?'

'We had to leave the country —'

'You're not a member of a terrorist group, are you?'

'No, sir. I'm a doctor, in fact.'

The officer starts writing something on another piece of paper.
'If you were a doctor, why did you have to leave Iran?' His tone is
harsh.

'Sir, it's complicated . . . I was arrested because I wrote some books
that were condemned by the Islamic regime, and I'm a Jew so —'

'You're a Jew, are you?' he interrupts me again. 'Why are you here, then? Turkey is a Muslim country. Why don't you go to Israel?' He stares at me.

'Sir, my wife is a Muslim and she doesn't wish to live in Israel.'

There's a heavy silence in the room. Niloofar starts crying and Azita asks the officer if she can sit down but he ignores her.

'You're not carrying any guns or drugs, are you?'

'No, sir.'

'You're not Kurdish?'

'No, sir.'

'Okay. We're going to keep all your passports and documents here and give you a piece of paper as your legal identification. If you leave Turkey we'll give your original ID back to you on the day of your departure. Now, listen to me.' He's looking at Azita and me intently. 'While you're here as asylum seekers, if you do anything wrong, and I mean *anything*, you will be deported immediately. Understand?'

'Yes, sir,' we both reply.

'You must go to the police station nearest to your accommodation and sign the registry every day, so we can make sure you're living in Ankara. And you're not allowed to work, study or travel anywhere in Turkey. Is that clear?'

'Yes, sir.'

'Dismissed!'

Degraded and fretful, we leave the office. Niloofar needs feeding and Newsha's in tears – she can feel the fear, shame and, worst of all, humiliation in her parents. I can't do anything except distract her, and I try telling her some lame, funny story. We sit down in a corner of the busy hall and wait another two hours for our *kimlik*, identification card, to be given to us.

We leave the building and after changing buses several times, by five o'clock we're looking for a place to stay in the suburb of Ulus. It's full of narrow, crowded, dusty streets, with a few ramshackle houses and some dodgy shops here and there. Dishevelled men are selling stolen items in the street: an old hairdryer, a rusty pair of pliers, a broken fan, worn-out pants and shirts. Everything is corroded and tarnished.

We find a cheap, old motel and pay for one night. The receptionist asks for ID when we check in and as I hand him our *kimlik* he says, 'Evsiz.'

In the morning I suggest to Azita we rent the room but she feels unsafe after drunk people yelled and walked up and down the corridors all night. The room is also in the worst position, right next to the toilets.

We decide to look for a rental together but have no idea where to start. We climb into buses going towards other cheap parts of Ankara. I walk the streets with tired little Newsha's hand in mine, and Azita's behind us with Niloofar in her arms. It's an extremely hot and humid day. I don't know how to say 'rent' or 'real estate' in Turkish so I look at all the shop signs for clues. I finally find a real estate agent but as soon as I start talking the man realises I'm an *evsiz* and hurries me out.

By two in the afternoon we're exhausted, so I buy three boiled eggs and a piece of bread and we sit in some shade to eat our lunch. When we set off again, I spot the two Iranian men who were following us in the bazaar. These men can't accidentally be in Istanbul and then in Ankara. I keep an eye on them using a concealed dentist's mirror in my sleeve, which I worked with while spying for MOIS. I don't say anything to Azita as I know she'd panic.

The next real estate agent is kind and tries to talk to us. When he realises what we're after he shakes his head and says, 'Kefil.' I don't know what he means.

At seven in the evening we catch a minibus back to the motel in Ulus, fatigued and frustrated. That night I hardly sleep, wondering whether the two Iranian agents will harm me and my family. I think about my mother, who has no idea where we are or what's happened to us.

In the morning our ordeal begins again on another scorching day. We try a few different areas and end up on the outskirts of Ankara, where there are horrible, cheap houses but nothing for *evsizs* to rent.

We decide to return to the UN tomorrow to get advice from Iranians who've spent more time in Turkey. We have to find an affordable room because we're paying twenty dollars a night at this motel, a rate I'm sure is much higher for us than for Turks.

In front of the UN building we speak to a young Iranian man called Payam, who's been in Turkey for three years. 'I took part in a demonstration at Tehran University against the regime and was kicked out of uni. They arrested five of my classmates – I was lucky to escape. The UN officer interviewed me last year and I'm still waiting for my results.'

I see the grief and disappointment on Payam's face and feel sorry for him. He then notices Newsha and Niloofar and says sympathetically, 'At least I'm single. You have a wife and two little kids.'

'I must find a place to stay, Payam. What should I do?'

'Go to the real estate offices. It took me seven months but I now share a room with an Iranian family. Before this I slept in the streets many nights.'

'How do you say house in Turkish?' I ask him.

'"Ev".'

'How do I ask for a house to rent?'

'Just say "Ev var?", which means "Is there a house?" They'll know what you mean.'

'Someone said something about a kefil.'

'Yes, you'll need a guarantor, a Turkish person who's a public servant and is willing to guarantee you.'

I look at him in despair. Finding such a person is likely to be impossible. As we walk away Payam says, 'Try Dikmen. You'll have more luck there.'

Within an hour we're in the suburb of Dikmen. It seems more prosperous than Ulus, with proper houses and ordinary shops, and there are a lot of real estate agents because it's a newer suburb.

In the first office we try, there are three men playing backgammon.

'Ev var?' I ask them.

They turn to look at us. One of them says something I don't understand and waves us out. We go to more than six real estate offices without any luck, until in the afternoon we walk into one at the end of a long street. It's a comparatively nice room with air conditioning. I would love to sit for a few minutes, just to cool down. There's a man in his early twenties with a ponytail and jeans. I ask him if he speaks English.

'Yes. How can I help you?' An older man, who I assume is his boss, is quietly watching us but I'm relieved I can at least talk to someone.

'Listen, brother, I'm a doctor from Iran. This is my wife and children, and we've been looking for a room to rent for two days. No one seems to be able to help us. We can't sleep in the street, and my youngest is only two months old and she's getting dehydrated. Do you have somewhere we can stay?'

The young man stares at us. I'm so apprehensive he's going to turn us away. Finally he says, 'Come with me,' and leaves the office.

When we're outside he asks how much money we have.

'I couldn't bring much with me, but we don't care what kind of room it is. We just need a roof over our heads. Please, brother, please.'

The young man nods. 'Okay, wait here.' He goes back inside and says something to the older man, then comes out again and directs us to follow him.

He walks over to a red Fiat, opens the door and gets in. We stand in the street, watching him.

'Come on. Yallah,' he says.

I sit in the front passenger seat and Azita and the kids are in the back. It feels so good to be in a normal car again, not a taxi or a bus, and I remember my brand-new silver Peugeot in Iran.

The young Turk says, 'That agency only has expensive units, so we're going to another one that has cheaper rooms.' It only takes us ten minutes to get there. When the car stops he says, 'Listen, don't bring your family. We're going to say that the room is just for you, okay?'

'Sure.' I ask Azita to stay in the car with the children. Before entering this other agency, which has a much smaller office, the young man pauses and holds out his hand. 'I'm Bulent.'

'Hi, Bulent. I'm Kooshyar.' And I shake his hand vigorously.

Bulent goes into the office and I follow nervously. He talks to an elderly man at the desk and after a few minutes I hear 'kefil' again. My heart sinks. But Bulent says something to the old man, who then opens a drawer and gives Bulent a set of keys. I cannot believe my eyes.

'Let's go and see this room,' Bulent says to me.

'Thank you, Bulent. God bless you.'

After a fifteen-minute drive we stop at a five-storey complex. 'Here it is,' Bulent exclaims as he steps out of the car.

The building is old and unimpressive, and is shaped like a tall man doubled over in pain. Most of its windows are broken. Bulent uses one of the keys to open the main door and when he opens it I can see stairs going up and down. I'm hoping he'll go up, but instead he goes downstairs and we follow him. The staircase becomes darker and damper as we walk three storeys down. I grew up in basements in Iran, but never as deep as this.

Finally we reach the bottom. It sounds like the earth's core. 'That's the heating engine!' Bulent shouts, pointing to an enormous machine rattling loudly. Next to it is a small door, which Bulent opens using another key. We enter and see two rooms and a small bathroom with a hose hanging from the roof instead of a shower. It looks like a fishing rod bending from the pull of a gigantic stingray.

'This is it,' he says.

The room is noisy, gloomy and extremely humid, and the murky bathroom stinks, but we're so grateful to have it.

The rent is fifty dollars a fortnight and I agree to a three-month lease. On the way back to the office I ask Bulent about the *kefil*.

He says, 'It's okay. I already told him I would guarantee you.'

I'm so grateful for Bulent's compassion. 'But you don't even know me.'

'I trust you, Kooshyar. I've lived a life that allows me to distinguish good from bad.'

An hour later, after signing the paperwork and paying four weeks' rent, we say goodbye to Bulent. I offer him some money but he refuses.

Three hours later we've moved into our new home in Dikmen, putting our small amount of luggage and few belongings on the concrete floor. It's ten o'clock at night and we're all so exhausted we don't care where we are. I try the toilet and realise it's just a hole in the floor with no seat. Azita puts Niloofar on her outstretched legs and rocks her until she goes to sleep. I lie down next to Newsha and roll my shirt into a pillow for her. She closes her big brown eyes and after I've told her a story about a little boy who loved pigeons, and who flew into the air with seven birds and reached paradise, she too falls asleep.

At eleven-thirty Azita and I are still talking about our grim future in Turkey when we're startled by a knock on the door. I panic – it must be the Iranian agents.

'Stay here,' I tell Azita. I walk cautiously over to the door and ask, 'Who is it?'

'It's me. Bulent.'

I open the door slowly and see him with a woman in her fifties. He steps inside and introduces the woman as his mother.

We say hello and the woman looks at Newsha and Niloofar lying on the concrete floor. She seems concerned and whispers something in Turkish to Bulent. 'My mother wants to know if you have any bedding,' he says.

We shake our heads in embarrassment. 'But we're okay. I'll find something to sleep on later,' I say.

Bulent's mother says something to him again. 'We'll be back soon,' he says, and they leave.

Half an hour later they return with a mattress, two small blankets and four pillows. Bulent's mother is carrying a bag and hands it to Azita with a smile. It contains a few small shirts and skirts for Newsha.

'Thank you so much. Thank you,' Azita says, and then bursts into tears. Bulent's mother hugs her and says something in Turkish.

'My mother says these clothes were my sister's when she was little. She wants you to know she's happy to help anytime,' says Bulent.

I'm frozen in astonishment. 'You are angels,' I whisper to Bulent and his lovely mother.

After they've gone, and Azita and the girls are all in a deep sleep, I sit down in a corner. I'm absolutely fatigued and emotionally shattered. I cry silently for a long time.

SIX

The next day I catch two different minibuses, the cheapest but slowest mode of transport in Turkey, to sign the register at the nearest police station. When I arrive the officer at the front desk is reading a magazine and completely ignores me. I stand there for five minutes, unsure of what to do, then eventually say, 'Sir.'

He continues reading, so I say it again more loudly.

He finally looks up. 'Iranian?' he asks harshly.

When I nod he points at a pen on the desk in front of me, which also has a large book open on it. Many names from other countries are written in it, some of which I recognise as Iranian. The officer says something in Turkish I don't understand. I guess he wants me to sign the book so I write my name and date it.

When I put the pen down the officer shakes his head and goes back to his magazine. The whole experience makes me feel humiliated, and I curse Azita: without her stubbornness we would be in Israel by now.

It takes me more than an hour to return to our basement in Dikmen. When I get back Azita tells me we need to set up a kitchen because buying takeaway food is expensive. I promise to find something but I have no idea how. What I do know is that when our money runs out, we're doomed.

I buy a secondhand, undoubtedly stolen, prepaid mobile phone for five dollars in Ulus, which I plan to use only for vital calls. Though it costs more than ten dollars a minute to ring Iran, I have to make sure my mother is safe. She's shocked when she hears my voice – she can't believe I'm still alive.

'What are you doing in Turkey? They told me you were in jail. They told me you were going to be hanged.' I know she's talking about MOIS. 'They took me and kept me there for ten days. They interrogated me . . .' she says, sobbing.

'I'm sorry, Maman jan. I just wanted you to know I'm fine. I have to go now, but I'll call you again soon.'

I hang up. I can't ask her about her interrogation or tell her more about myself as phones are tapped in Iran.

The next day I go to Ulus again to find more cheap stolen items, and buy an old pot and some ancient spoons and plates. I also get some electrical elements to make a kind of stove. At university I studied physics, maths and electronics (as well as history and mythology) as much as I studied medicine. I also worked in electronics for many years in Iran, including in Reza Frekans' radio repair shop where I made a crystal radio at the age of nine.

I return again the following day to look for a fridge. The salesman is Izhak, an Assyrian Iranian man in his thirties who's been in Turkey for seven years. His ethnicity delights me because one of my books deals with the history of the Assyrians, who ruled the Middle East and Mesopotamia almost three and a half thousand years ago, prior to the Persian Empire. Assyrians these days are mainly Christian and live in parts of Iran, Iraq and Syria, and they undergo much scrutiny because of their faith. Izhak works illegally in the fridge-repair shop while he waits for the UN to reopen his case. He scratches himself constantly and I feel great sympathy for him, knowing he probably isn't able to shower more than once a week. Izhak lives in perpetual anxiety and despair, knowing that he could be deported at any moment. I see my future in him.

He sells me a thirty-year-old fridge for five dollars instead of twenty. Later on I realise that Izhak has a lot of experience and knowledge about Turkey, refugees and the UN, so the next day I return to get some advice. Izhak tells me, 'Be careful. There are many con artists here who'll take advantage of your misery. Waiting for the UN is hard but if you have a real case and your life is in danger, they'll eventually support you.' I'm amazed Izhak is so optimistic after what he's been through. At the end of our conversation I feel a glimmer of hope.

The following day Izhak takes me to his house after work. It's an awful unit in downtown Ankara: a single underground room and an outside toilet. It reminds me of where I lived as a child – we also never saw daylight or felt the breeze. Izhak's unit has a timber floor and when I look closer I can see fleas jumping around. I realise now why he's constantly scratching.

He offers me tea and a piece of bread. I ask him why he left

Iran, and he says it's because he'd converted to Christianity and could have been hanged for forsaking his 'true' religion. To me Izhak embodies true Christianity: he's risked his life for his faith, and he's a very kind man. He has an elderly mother in Iran to whom he sends a small amount of money every month. His story tears at my heart.

The next morning I visit Izhak again at his shop. Conversing with him is somehow comforting. While he's fixing an old fridge he tells me, 'There's a place called Saklamak Haneh run by Islamic hardliners in Turkey. They give one free meal a day to homeless Muslims. They might help you.'

Izhak has just written down the address when a sudden commotion breaks out around us. The police have come to arrest illegal workers. Sellers abandon their wares and run through the narrow alleyways between the makeshift shops, knocking things to the ground. Izhak drops everything and sprints. I watch him disappear down a lane and never see him again, this man who lives in poverty and dread because of his faith.

I decide to walk to Saklamak Haneh and find it in less than half an hour. In a large hall with metal benches a man is serving sticky rice from behind a counter. It's midday so there are a lot of people eating. The server has a thick torso and wide neck, and his bushy moustache reminds me of pubic hair. He has a conspicuous brownish blotch in the centre of his forehead, the result of years of pressing his forehead five times a day on *mohr* for prayer. *Mohr* is compressed, consecrated soil that symbolises Allah, and devout Shias go all the way to Najaf and Karbala in Iraq to get it. The more encrusted and prominent the forehead mark, the more pious the man. Pressing the head is quite important in Islam. Shias press harder than Sunnis, men harder than women. The chief in our slum, Mullah Mohamad, used to tie a hot rock on his forehead with a piece of cloth for many hours a day to get a nice round mark. His son Hassan, who left Iran and became a rap singer in Dubai, revealed the trick to my friend.

When I go to the counter the server asks me where I'm from. When I say 'Iran' he shakes his head. I try to explain I'm a registered asylum seeker but he still refuses to give me some food. It seems their generosity is reserved solely for Turkish citizens. Perhaps the charity was established by an Islamic political party as a means of gaining support; obviously an *evsiz* Iranian can't vote in the next Turkish election. Just before I turn away, an older man walks behind the counter and says something in Turkish to the server. I gather it's something like, 'Muslims are Muslims – it doesn't matter where they're from.' The server reluctantly gives me a small bowl of rice. I ask the older man if I can take home some food for my children but he says the facility is only for homeless people, who must eat on the premises, so I give back the bowl of rice and leave.

The next day I return to Saklamak Haneh with Azita and the children, and we wait for the older man to appear. Though he has no mark on his forehead, he has a kind heart. When I see him I go up to the counter with Newsha and Niloofar. He looks at them, the hunger obvious in their anxious eyes and pinched cheeks. He turns away and is silent for a moment. Then he says to me, 'Bring your pot with you every day and I'll give you food to take home.' This becomes our deal: I receive one free serve of rice every day from the Saklamak Haneh and take it home to share with my family. It is almost all we eat.

We've been living in the subterranean unit for two weeks when one night, at about one in the morning, there's a loud banging on our door. I look at Azita, who's panicking. She says not to open it but I get up and ask, 'Who is it?'

'Bulent. Open the door, Kooshyar! There's been an earthquake – get out now!' he shouts. We all rush from the building to see thousands of people in the streets. Bulent's fiancée, Funda, is in his car and we join her. We stay there, all jammed together, for hours. There's absolute chaos around us – people huddle in small groups wherever they can on the street or in cars. Throughout the night we occasionally feel tremors and we're very grateful for Bulent's Fiat.

For the next three weeks I watch the news on televisions in shop windows and see footage of towns that have been completely demolished. At least seventeen thousand people have been killed, nearly fifty thousand are injured and thousands more are missing. About half a million people are now homeless and the damage is about six and a half billion dollars. Yet we felt nothing in our unit deep in the ground.

The next week I go back to the UN to get more advice from asylum seekers gathered outside the building. The UN, the Turkish government and the police tell us nothing – like slum dwellers, asylum seekers don't exist in the eyes of the outside world. But talking to other refugees is tricky: much of the information might be incorrect, and it's dangerous for Iranian asylum seekers to divulge too much in case intelligence agents are nearby.

When I arrive the police are arresting someone for protesting. I see Shadi and Arya again. They've been thrown out of their tiny apartment because the landlord discovered they were sharing it, which is illegal, and they've been looking for new accommodation for days. I offer to share our place – such as it is – and they agree immediately, offering to pay half the rent. That same day they move into the other room of the unit. We're all happy because now at least we have people to talk to.

Though it's good to have company, our place is far from ideal. The two small rooms are only separated by a thin fibro wall. In the corner of our room the ceiling is covered in mildew and the single shower is cramped and mouldy. As well as the constant clamour of the heating engine, we can hear all the noises of the people in the units above us – walking, talking, snoring and sometimes yelling. One Turkish couple fight continually – the woman's deafening screams are punctuated by furniture smashing.

Nevertheless we sit and talk until late every night. It's all that's keeping us sane. We discuss everything, but mostly what happened to us in Iran and what may happen to us in Turkey. Most of our stories are full of heartbreak and disenchantment. One night when Arya is out meeting a friend, Shadi tells us why they left Iran.

'Arya divorced me three years ago and married another woman. He was just not interested in me anymore. Then I met a man, Ali, who I later found out was married. But, as you know, men can have more than one wife in Iran so I was seeing him a couple of times a week. I have a three-year-old son and a seven-year-old daughter from my marriage with Arya and they lived with me. Ali was very nice and would spend a lot of money on us. After a while he told me he was a Revolutionary Guard, and he introduced me to a fellow soldier, a friend of his who was a brutal man,' she says.

I know how ruthless these Revolutionary Guards are. They're above the law and have total authority to arrest, jail and execute people. They even fight in foreign 'jihad conflicts' against infidels. Everyone in Iran is terrified of them.

Shadi continues. 'The other man raped me. I was too scared to do anything.' She starts crying. 'After a while there were three men who would regularly rape me, sometimes at the same time. They were in the secret service and they'd take me to their safe house to do these horrible things to me. They could kill me if I tried to defend myself.

'Then one day Ali asked me to do a job for him, which he said would make a lot of money. I had to go to a dollar seller and ask to buy thousands of US dollars, pretending I was rich. When the man tried to sell them to me, Ali and the others would come in and arrest him.'

American currency exchange is controlled by the government and it's illegal for anyone to exchange US dollars in Iran.

'I did this many times and they arrested several people. The victims had to pay hefty fines to be released. But after almost two years Arya came back. He had separated from his second wife and we decided to live together again. Ali threatened to kill both of us.' Shadi sighs. 'That's why we left the kids with my parents in Mashhad and escaped to Turkey. Our interview at the UN is next month.' I'm horrified at Shadi's story, and can only imagine what it's like for her and Arya to be separated from their children.

Once a week they go to the telephone centre and call them. One day, because using my mobile phone to call Iran is expensive, I go with them to ring my mother. She's worried about me but I can't tell her anything, especially about going to the UN. I just say I'll come back to Iran soon, and that we're doing well in Turkey. She tells me the government has taken my house. This is the house that cost me a hundred and forty-five thousand dollars, a high price in Iran where home loans are practically non-existent.

I bought it a year before my arrest and spent months renovating it but didn't get a chance to enjoy it. Now I'm afraid that if the UN rejects our case, my children and Azita will be sent back to Iran without somewhere to live. If that happens, somehow I must stay in Turkey and work illegally, just like Izhak, until I get enough money to pay a people smuggler to get me to another country. From there I will apply to bring my family to live with me. This could all easily take several years.

My mother also tells me she's moved to Isfahan, where she was born, but her Jewish relatives haven't accepted her back into the family because she married a Muslim. Our Jewish family assume my brother and I are Muslims because of our father, while the Muslim side consider us Jewish because of our mother. So we belong nowhere.

Every night, while the others sleep, I sit and think in despair until dawn, looking at my traumatised and starving children and worrying we'll soon be separated. I don't know how they'd survive in Iran without me. I keep myself busy during the day by teaching Newsha the English alphabet and how to read and write simple letters. Bulent and Funda also relieve our isolation when they visit every now and then.

One night Azita and I, along with Shadi and Arya, go to the large supermarket nearby to buy bread and milk. For many weeks Newsha's been asking us to buy one of the colourful boxes of ice-cream in the shop but we can't afford them. When we go back to our unit, though, I surprise everyone by producing a box of chocolate ice-cream I've managed to steal. Everyone cheers and we sit around the ice-cream box, digging in with our crooked, rusty spoons. I watch Newsha as she eats, her eyes shining with pleasure.

All the anxiety has lifted from her face and her small hand grips the spoon with a vitality and determination I haven't seen for a long time. Here we are in a slum, surrounded by noise and dirt and with nothing but a few shabby belongings, but for one precious moment it's as if we're in paradise.

The Turkish police still treat me with disdain when I sign the book each day. In the afternoons I walk Newsha and Niloofar to a small park so they can play on the slide or swing and try to forget about our situation. Some Turkish people there look at us suspiciously and are possessive about the play equipment. One day when Newsha is on the swing a Turkish boy and his mother come over and tell her to get off, calling her an *evsiz*. She's quite upset when I lead her away so I tell her 'evsiz' means 'Iranian' and is not a bad word.

On the way to the park we pass a big grocery. Out the front a man sells fruit from a few boxes, probably paying rent to the shop owner to allow him to have his small business there. Each time we walk past him Newsha stares at the large peaches, apples and oranges. The peaches are almost a dollar each but they're so ripe and tempting.

We don't have enough money to buy luxuries such as fruit. I can't remember the last time I had an orange or an apple. The only thing we purchase each day is a loaf of bread to eat with the bowl of rice from Saklamak Haneh. I follow Saeed's advice and change my money into Turkish lira daily, converting as little as possible. The word 'zam' is one of the first I learned here: it means inflation. When the cost of bread rises a few cents every day, the seller shrugs his shoulders and says, 'Zam.'

One day while we're walking past the fruit boxes Newsha stops, stares at the peaches, and says she wants one. I kneel down next to her and say I'll buy one for her soon but not today. Suddenly the fruit seller picks up a big juicy peach, sits beside Newsha and offers it to her, saying in Turkish, 'Here, sweetheart.' She's too shy to accept it but he grabs her hand, places the peach in it and pats her hair. Newsha looks at me.

'Take it, baba, and say thank you.' Newsha whispers 'thank you' to the seller and we go to the park. I think, There are plenty of nice people in Turkey. It's a very poor country but I'm impressed by how democratic it is. I can see how free the people are and that religion is separate from the constitution. Though Turkey has many Muslim hardliners who want to take control of the government, the majority are pro-democracy and secular. Music, writing, art, fashion and the media are significantly more relaxed than they are in Iran and I hope that one day this model is applied throughout the entire Middle East.

There's still another two weeks until our UN interview but my anxiety is sky-high. All the other Iranian asylum seekers I've spoken to have been rejected. However, I notice a lot of them are here for economic reasons – they simply have a difficult life in Iran and want to go to a more affluent country. Many pretend to be dissidents who've opposed the regime, but UN officers have in-depth knowledge of Iran and its prisons so they know immediately that these stories are false.

One day in front of the UN I meet a young Iranian man who tells me he participated in student demonstrations in Tehran, and that if he's deported he'll be arrested. He shows me a large scar on his arm. 'See this? The police bashed me when I was protesting for regime change.'

I look at his scar. It's easily at least ten years old. I tell him that, and he laughs. 'Yes, I got this when I fell off my bike.' He admits he had no real problems in Iran – he wants to go to the US just to drink alcohol and have fun in nightclubs.

I also meet four women who are part of the People's Mojahedin, a Marxist–Islamic group that opposes the Iranian regime. I know the organisation well: two of my friends were executed for being members. All four women are aged between twenty and thirty-two. Their UN interview was fourteen months ago. Though they've escaped from Iran, many of their comrades have been jailed or executed.

A week before our interview we're invited by Ziba, the head of the group, to their house. They live in a slum on the outskirts of Ankara, on the top floor of an old two-storey house, and it takes us almost two hours to get there by bus. Ziba tells me about their activities in Iran. I admire their courage, and am disappointed the UN is likely to reject all their cases because of Mojahedin's increasingly armed resistance in recent years. The conversation bores Newsha, who asks if she can go outside and play with the children in the street, and we let her go.

Ziba tells me her group is working on exposing Iran's nuclear weapons program. I knew the Shah had a nuclear program, but after the revolution it was cancelled. Ziba's group say they have evidence the Islamic regime is developing a nuclear bomb to blackmail Israel and the West, and that Iranian scientists have been receiving secret nuclear training in Pakistan. In 1989 the Revolutionary Army received their first centrifuge assemblies, and in 1995 more than two thousand components and subassemblies were shipped to Iran.

'If they get their hands on nuclear weapons,' I say, 'nowhere on this planet would be safe.'

'I know. This is what we're trying to tell the UN.'

Suddenly Newsha returns, crying. She tells me that a much bigger Turkish boy has pushed her off the swing. I examine her arm and assure her it's just bruised. When we finish talking with Ziba and the other People's Mojahedin women, I wish them luck. On the bus going home I wonder, If these warriors against the Iranian regime are likely to be rejected by the UN, what are our chances?

We arrive back at four. By six Newsha is in agony, so we go by bus to the hospital at Hacettepe. The emergency department is overcrowded and we have to wait hours before we're seen. When the doctor finally gets to us the first thing he says is, 'You're not Turkish citizens, are you?'

'No, we're asylum seekers.' I show him our UN papers.

'In that case you have to pay sixty-five dollars for the consultation and the X-ray.'

'Okay, that's fine.' This amount is equal to one month's living expenses, but I would give my heart for Newsha. Once I've paid, the doctor starts examining her arm and when he puts the X-ray on the light box my heart sinks. Her bone has snapped in half. I hug Newsha in my arms. 'Can you give her something for the pain, please?'

'First she has to be seen by the orthopaedic registrar,' he replies as he walks away.

Half an hour later a young orthopaedic registrar comes to us and looks at the X-ray. He realises we're asylum seekers and I tell him I used to be a doctor. Thankfully he speaks reasonably good English.

'I'm going to apply a cast but I won't charge you for that,' he says.

'Thank you so much.' The kind-hearted orthopod gives Newsha some pain relief and explains she needs to wear the cast for at least four weeks. By midnight we're finally home and Newsha falls asleep immediately. I sit and watch her sleeping, tears blurring my eyes.

I can't stop thinking about my UN interview. I know I'm honest and my story is true, but how will they know that? How can they verify what happened to me? I don't blame the UN for being sceptical about asylum seekers when so many people fabricate their stories, but how do people who are genuinely in danger prove their case?

Later on I ring my mother on my mobile but she doesn't answer. I just want to hear her voice, to make sure she's okay. I feel dread in the pit of my stomach – maybe she's been taken by MOIS. I try again in the afternoon and then once more the following morning, but still she doesn't pick up. It's very out of character. I'm extremely concerned but I need to stay calm and focus on my interview. The lives of my children are at stake. Besides, I know there's nothing I can do to help her.

I decide to go back once again to the crowd outside the UN building. As usual there are a large number of asylum seekers around the building. I approach an Iranian-looking man in his thirties and start talking to him. His name is Dariush and he came to Turkey with his wife fourteen months ago. Not long after they arrived, while they were waiting for their interview, his wife became pregnant. Two months later they had their interview, with a French UN officer.

'She's a butcher – she has no compassion,' Dariush tells me. 'I explained I was arrested for writing an article in an opposition newspaper. I told her I was detained for four months, the newspaper was shut down, and when I was released I wasn't allowed to have any government job. Basically, I had a black mark against my name and no one would hire me, so we decided to leave Iran.' He pauses and then says, 'Sometimes I'm so frightened, I wish we'd never left. This is worse than being in jail.'

Dariush's story sounds genuine. But his heartbreak didn't end there. 'A few months ago, after our daughter was born, my wife got sick. I took her to hospital and they discovered she has a rare form of cancer that develops after pregnancy.' He's talking about choriocarcinoma, which is very aggressive: the chance of survival beyond six months is virtually zero.

Dariush shakes his head. 'It's been almost a year since I had my interview with that French officer. I've sent them the paperwork showing my wife's grave situation but they have no mercy. They still won't tell me the result of my interview.'

I also speak to a 22-year-old man from Tehran called Babak. He tells me he went to that Turkish lawyer, Mr Kamal, to prepare his case and paid him four thousand dollars – his father's savings after working for twenty years as a teacher. 'Kamal is a crook. He claims he used to work for the UN and knows everything about it but he's full of shit. He said that if I told the UN officer I'm gay my case would be successful. But in the interview I was asked to give details about having sex with another man. And, as you can imagine, I wasn't convincing.' Babak smiles bitterly.

I'm still cautious about being followed so I give everyone a vague story about myself, simply saying I'm an author who got into trouble with the government. Another man, Morad, who's been waiting for his interview results for two years, asks me if I have any documents to show I was arrested.

'I have a copy of some of my books, but nothing else.'

'That's nothing,' Morad says. 'I have an original document from the jail, from when I was given three days' leave. I showed it to them but it wasn't enough.'

I can't find anyone who's been successful, and I realise that even if my interview goes well, it'll take more than a year to get the results and then several more months after that to be sent to a new country.

'I knew a woman who was successful last year,' says Kamran, another asylum seeker. 'After eighteen months the UN sent her to Norway, a frozen hell. She was devastated.'

'So you don't have any choice even if your case is accepted?' I ask.

Kamran shakes his head. 'Are you kidding? The UN isn't a travel agency. You could end up in Iceland!'

It's not hard to see why asylum seekers approach people smugglers.

SEVEN

In the summer of 1992 I was on my way to a lecture at Tehran University, walking down Valiasr Street. This is the longest street in the entire Middle East, and its southern end is close to the slum I grew up in. Running for almost 18 kilometres, Valiasr Street connects the north of the city and the south, massive villas and shantytowns, modern civilisation and ancient Persia, those who embrace Western values and the fanatical militiamen who oppose them. There are some eighteen thousand sycamore trees on the street, although most of them are at the northern end.

Tehran has some bizarre street and place names. There's Execution Square, a famous large square in the middle of a round-about. Khaled Eslamboli Street is named for the assassin who murdered Anwar Sadat, the Egyptian president, after he signed a peace agreement with Israel in 1981. The main square in south Tehran is called Shush Square – so much for freedom of speech. There's also a Jihad Street, a Jihad Square and an Islamic Jihad Foundation in every town.

I eventually reached the university, where Mr Naseri, a publisher and history academic, was giving a lecture about his pro-monarchist views, ideas that could have had him publicly hanged. While he spoke I remembered my father's reaction when the Shah went into exile on 16 January 1979. I'd never seen my father cry: not when his mother passed away, not even when his youngest son from his first wife died suddenly from a ruptured brain aneurysm. But while he watched the Shah kiss the soil then climb the steps into the aeroplane, my father sobbed. At that moment I became a monarchist.

Two months after Mr Naseri's lecture I became a formal member of a subversive monarchist party with its headquarters in London. I knew that by joining I was significantly endangering my life but I couldn't resist a chance to fight for a better Iran: for democracy, for freedom of speech and of the media, for human rights. Almost a hundred thousand people had been executed since the Islamic regime came to power, and I could no longer stay silent.

Out of the group's hundreds of members across Iran I was introduced to only four, who all lived in Mashhad. There were no written notes or tape recordings of our meetings, which happened once a month in one of our houses. Our chief was Mr Naseri, and our mission was simple: to gather support for a monarchy similar to the European model, with a prime minister elected by the people and the monarch being a unifying figurehead. Because everyone knew how corrupt the last king had been – jailing and punishing his opponents – we had to convince Iranians there's no conflict between a monarchy and a democracy. We also wanted to remind them of the Islamic regime's crimes, and advocate for separating government and religion.

In our meetings we'd discuss how we could subtly approach people to talk to them about our views. We'd also create flyers and work out ways to distribute them; this latter part was the most dangerous aspect of our mission. We knew that if we were caught, we'd be tortured to death. According to our instructions, if one of us was arrested he had to resist for twenty-four hours to give the rest time to escape. Between meetings we made sure no one had been captured by calling each other then hanging up every second evening just before midnight. Four calls meant the group was intact; three meant one of us had been caught, and we'd all have to disappear. If we had to cancel a meeting, or if the group was in danger, we'd mail coded letters to each other, the post being safer than any form of electronic communication.

We memorised the number of the head office in London. We knew each other's names and membership numbers but never used them. The four other members of my cell were single university students. Six months after joining I was assigned to be the leader of our small group and felt great responsibility for the safety of these remarkable young men. When I saw the hope and passion in their eyes, I could feel our country move closer towards freedom, justice and democracy.

Though we took turns hosting the meetings, we never met at my house because Azita knew nothing about my involvement with the group. I knew that if she found out she would beg me to divorce her. Azita was already appalled by my Jewish faith and fed up with the risks my writing entailed, and would refuse to tolerate any further stress. Sadly, even without meeting any Jew other than me in her entire life, Azita sincerely believed ridiculous myths about Jewish women kidnapping little Muslim boys, severing their heads and drinking their blood.

It's not long until my UN interview and I am thinking about contacting my monarchist group's headquarters in London. I don't tell anyone about this, not even Azita.

'If you end up escaping Iran, contact the head office,' said Mr Naseri when we last met. 'They'll protect you and get you to a safe country.'

Since going into hiding, I haven't heard what's happened to the rest of my group. I hope they're okay – I haven't said a word about their identity. When I was kidnapped in February 1997 MOIS knew I supported the idea of a monarchy, and that from the age of ten I'd read forbidden books, but they didn't know about my involvement in the monarchist group. Though they were aware of our meetings, they thought I was teaching literature during them. They had no idea about my relationship with Mr Naseri, other than that he published one of my books.

A couple of weeks ago I heard from other asylum seekers that the UN supported members of peaceful opposition groups, but I wasn't sure it was true. After a lot of thought, though, I decide to seek help from the party I've risked my life to support. It's seven o'clock in the morning and Azita has fallen asleep again after dealing with Niloofar, who cried all night with what seemed to be abdominal cramps. I sneak out of the house, walk for a few minutes and then stand on a corner. The street is quiet. I take out my prepaid mobile phone, insert the SIM card and call the head office. As it rings, I look around anxiously.

'Good morning, Karmel Bakery, Steve speaking.'

I hang up. I must've dialled the wrong number. I try again but the same man answers the phone. I hang up immediately, disappointed and betrayed. It seems we've been given false information. What if the whole organisation was fake? What if it was a trap? But that can't be the case, because in all their torture MOIS never mentioned my monarchist activities. Maybe I've mixed up the number due to all the recent stress. I decide to dial again and talk to the man this time.

'Hi Steve, my name's Kooshyar and I'm calling from Turkey. I am a member of the party and they gave me this number to ring when I got out of Iran.'

He hesitates for a few seconds.

'Hello? Are you still there?' I ask.

'Yes, Kooshyar, yes.' I can now hear a hint of a Persian accent in his words.

'Is this the right number?'

'Yes it is,' he says. I feel relieved knowing we haven't been deceived.

'Can you help me, please? I fled Iran three months ago and I need to get to a safe place.'

Steve asks for my full name and membership details, as well as my phone number in Turkey. After I've given these to him, he promises someone will contact me in half an hour.

While I wait, I pace up and down the streets of Dikmen. I worry that Azita has woken up and is looking for me but I can't let her know about this.

Finally, after fifty minutes of anxiety, my mobile phone rings.

'Mr Kooshyar Karimi?' It's a different man. 'My name is Kasra and I'm in charge of recruitment for the party. I understand that you have fled Iran. Can you tell me a bit more about your situation, please?'

I explain my story and he assures me he'll do what he can to help me. Then he asks for my special code, which was given to Mr Naseri by one of the organisation's secret agents. I tell him this as well as my date and place of birth.

'Thank you. Now can you tell me the name of the person who introduced you to the party? I know this must be frustrating for you but I have to make sure I'm talking to the right person, for the safety of the other members.'

'I understand. It was Mr Morteza Naseri, the history lecturer at Tehran University who published my most recent book. He introduced me in 1992 and soon afterwards I became the leader of a cell of five in Mashhad.'

'And what are the names of at least two of your members?'

I give him this information, and then there's silence. I panic for a second that I'm revealing too much to this unknown man on the other end of the line. But I have no choice – I have to trust him.

'Dr Karimi, I know about you and I'm pleased to tell you none of your team members have been captured.'

'Thank God for that,' I say.

'Now, what steps have you already taken in Turkey to move to another country?'

'I have an interview at the UNHCR soon.'

'That's good but as you probably know that process takes some

KOOSHYAR KARIMI

time. I'll send them a fax tomorrow confirming your membership and outlining your activities for the party. Because we're non-violent, the UN fully supports us so this fax will help your case significantly.'

'What should I say in the interview?' I ask.

'Just be honest. Tell them the truth about everything that's happened to you. I know the majority of cases in Turkey are rejected but yours is different. I can assure you that with our fax you'll have a great chance of being approved.'

'Thank you so much, Mr Kasra, thank you.' I feel buoyant with gratitude and joy.

'Okay, now listen. It's critical you keep this confidential, as you did in Iran. Turkey is not safe for you. You must not tell anyone about this, not a single soul, not even your family. Is that clear?'

'Yes.'

'Good. Unfortunately we can't provide any financial support, though we truly appreciate your efforts for the party. But we can definitely assist with your interview.'

'I'm not expecting any money. All I'm asking for is help getting us somewhere safe – anywhere.'

'I understand, Dr Karimi. I'll make sure the fax is sent by tomorrow, and I'll call you in two weeks to see how your interview went. Please stay calm and focused. Be safe.'

I walk back to our basement, feeling for the first time since leaving Iran that I'm not completely alone in this battle to find freedom for myself and my family.

Time passes so slowly. I wish I could tell Azita we now have outside support. She's accusing me daily of getting her and the children into this mess.

'Just give me another few days,' I say. 'If our interview with the UNHCR goes wrong, you go back to Iran with the girls and I'll stay here until I find a way out. I don't want you to suffer – it's me they want, after all.' She seems less furious, at least for a while, even though we both know that returning to Iran will be extremely difficult without our house to live in.

Two days before my interview I'm too nervous to stay in our unit so I go out for some air. It's a cold autumn day and I walk quickly down Dikmen Street. These days I keep the SIM card in my phone all the time, in case I receive a call from the party. I'm not far from home when my phone suddenly rings. 'Dr Karimi?' says a man's voice.

'Yes, who is this?'

'My name is Keeyan. I am Mr Kasra's superior in the party. I understand you have an interview in two days with the UNHCR, and that we've already sent them a fax confirming your brave work for us. But you will need to take some important documents with you to the interview, including your membership card, and these have been sent by registered post to our safe house in Ankara. I want you to go to the Sohoolo Hotel in Sohoolo Mahalasi, room 121, tomorrow at three and meet Jahan, our trusted agent there. He'll give you the documents.'

I go back to the basement elated, but feeling like an idiot for not contacting the party earlier. Finally I will have physical evidence to prove my claims.

When I leave the house the next day I tell Azita I'm going to the police headquarters to sign the register, and I'm not lying. But after signing the book I jump on a bus and go to the Sohoolo Hotel, in the centre of Ankara. I take the lift to the third level, find room 121 and knock on the door.

'Who is it?' someone asks from inside.

'Kooshyar Karimi.'

The door is opened by a man with prominent pointy ears and a thick moustache. His face is covered in so many zits and scars it reminds me of an omelette. 'Come in,' he says in Turkish. The room is quite large and bright and is decorated with modern furniture. He gestures for me to sit opposite another man, in his late thirties, sitting on a couch. There is a glossy black coffee table between us. I can't see the documents anywhere, and begin to feel uneasy.

'Dr Karimi, nice to see you,' says the man on the couch, in Farsi. 'My name is Attaran, and I'm here to help you. Let me explain the situation.' He takes a deep breath and leans forward so I look directly into his fierce eyes.

'I work for the Islamic intelligence service, and I know everything about you, Dr Karimi.'

Panic grips me. How stupid I was to come here. The man who claimed to be Mr Kasra's superior must have been a MOIS agent.

'Don't worry, we're not going to hurt you, as long as you cooperate just as you did in Iran. By the way, Samadi said hello,' he says, grinning.

Hearing the name of my torturer makes my heart sink. 'What exactly do you want from me?' These people could kill me in this room and nobody would ever know.

Attaran reaches into his pocket, takes out a mobile phone and dials a number. He looks at me. 'Have you been in contact with your mother, Dr Karimi?' he asks.

'I've tried but she hasn't answered the phone.' My voice is trembling.

'Yes, it's Attaran, put her on now,' he says, talking into the phone.

Then he puts it on the coffee table and turns on the speaker.

A man's voice says harshly, 'Talk now. Your son is on the other end of the line.'

Then I hear a woman's voice. 'Kooshyar jan, can you hear me?'

Attaran indicates to me to answer.

'Yes, Maman jan, I'm here. Are you okay?' I ask. My heart is pounding hard.

'Kooshyar jan, listen to me carefully. I am in custody. You have to do as I tell you or you will never see me again. Do you understand?' my mother says, her voice shaking.

'Yes.' I'm fighting back tears. I hate to think what might be happening to her.

'I'm told you're going to have an interview with the UN. Be very careful. If you tell them anything about that party, you will bury me. Is that clear?'

I'm horrified that by contacting the party, I've exposed them to MOIS. I have no idea how. It's almost impossible the intelligence service tapped my prepaid mobile here in Turkey. Maybe they used an extremist Islamic group in London to tap the party's line there. Whichever way, MOIS is now using my mother as a hostage to subdue the regime's biggest enemy: monarchists who are supported financially and politically by the West.

'Okay, Maman jan, I won't say anything to the UNHCR about the party. Nothing.'

'Promise?'

'I promise, Maman jan.' And the phone disconnects.

Attaran puts the mobile back in his pocket. 'Dr Karimi, I think you now understand the situation. If you talk about that goddamn party in your interview, your mother will not live another day. When they ask you about the fax, you are to tell them it's fake. Also, you are not to say anything about the thirteen Jews under arrest in Iran. If you play smart with us again, Murat will make sure your daughters are taken care of.' He points at the Turkish man who let me in.

The threat against my children fills me with rage, but I know I'm powerless.

'What do you want from me? Why don't you leave me alone? I'm nobody now,' I say desperately.

'I have told you what we want from you. Now you can go.'

The hulking Turk opens the door for me and I stumble over with shaking knees. I'm in shock, realising how truly fragile our safety is in Turkey. Then it hits me – I've endangered Mr Naseri and the two other members I named over the phone. I feel sick.

I meander through the streets for a long time before I'm able to think clearly again. I consider going to the UN or the police but I know they won't do anything to help yet another asylum seeker. Plus, by the time I've gone to the authorities, they will find no trace of Mr Attaran.

On the bus back to Dikmen I feel utterly vulnerable. When I get home I go straight to Niloofar and Newsha, pick them up and hold them against my chest.

'Are you okay?' asks Azita. 'You're crying.'

'Yes, I'm fine. Just a bit stressed about the interview tomorrow.'

And I press my face into my daughters' warm bodies, willing it to be true.

EIGHT

Later on Azita and I are talking about the interview when she says, 'By the way, something bizarre happened today.'

I'm instantly alert. 'What?'

'Arya and Shadi left early this afternoon with their bags, and they rang an hour later to say they've found a different place to live. Isn't that strange? I don't know how they organised something so quickly, or why they didn't even bother to say goodbye.'

I have a feeling it relates to what happened to me today, but I don't want to make Azita's anxiety worse. 'Don't worry, maybe they wanted to be somewhere less noisy. Good luck to them. We have more important things to be worried about.'

Azita asks me again, 'Have you practised saying your case?

I don't want you to sound confused or unsure.'

'Yes, a million times. But they'll double-check everything with you, so make sure you have the dates right too. If there's any discrepancy they'll reject us.'

'I'm sure you can convince them. Stay positive,' she says, but I can see how nervous she is.

'Azita,' I say seriously, 'if my interview is unsuccessful I want you to take the kids back to Iran. We don't have enough money to stay here for a long time and I don't want my children to suffer because of me.'

Azita nods. 'But what would you do?'

'I don't know, but I'll survive and somehow get to another country one day. Then you and the girls can join me.' Actually uttering these words is like being deeply sliced with a knife. 'It might take many years but we'll see each other again.'

Azita goes to sleep but I cannot rest. I look at Niloofar's plump lips and long black eyelashes, at Newsha's silky hair and angelic face. My heart aches. I try to imagine them happy and healthy in a new country. I won't let them grow up suffering the same hardships I did. Though they're here because of me, I have to hold on to the hope that everything I've done, and all they've sacrificed, will be worthwhile in the end.

Finally it's time to wake Azita. We change Niloofar's nappy and go out. I'm trying to remain calm. At eight o'clock we're in front of the UN building – the last hope for people who have nothing to lose. Regardless of whether we've left our homelands because of political or economic reasons, all of us have one thing in common: we've been crushed by the hammer of religion and tradition. We are the sacrificial goats of ancient, wretched cultures that seek blood constantly.

As usual there are many people there, gossiping, arguing, spying. Time passes slowly until nine o'clock, when the gate is opened by three guards who start calling out names. One by one couples and families go through the gate. The slow progression reminds me of Jews walking to the Nazi furnaces. The asylum seekers are body-searched before being guided inside. Finally my name is called.

I take a deep breath and go forward. One guard starts checking Azita and another one searches me. He points at my suitcase. 'What's in that?'

'Books,' I tell him.

The guard shakes his head. 'You can't take it inside. Only documents are allowed.'

'But sir, these are my documents.'

He takes the suitcase from me and orders us to go in. Azita starts begging him to give it back but there's no point. The first thing an asylum seeker loses is their dignity; the second is their voice.

After being ushered inside a large hall with yellow carpet, we sit down and look around. There are five other families and everyone seems very tense. Off the hall are five interview rooms. A Turkish woman hands out pamphlets to the adults and coloured pencils to the children. She shows us a small area for kids and says in Turkish, 'They can stay here and colour the pictures but they have to be quiet or we will send you all out.' Then she looks at the adults and says, 'You're not allowed to talk to each other. If you need to go to the toilet, ask the guards and they will take you there.'

Newsha joins a little Iranian boy and they start drawing and colouring in. Niloofar falls asleep on Azita's lap. Azita asks me if I'm okay and I nod. I feel as if I'm about to be interrogated and tortured again.

Soon an officer appears and announces someone's name. A man in his thirties stands up and follows him to one of the interview rooms. Time passes as slowly as a tortoise in mud. After half an hour another man is called into another room, then half an hour later a woman is called in. Newsha wants to go out so we try to distract her. Niloofar has started crying and Azita calms her down by feeding her.

The first asylum seeker comes out of the interview room after an hour and a half. His face is covered in sweat and he seems very distressed. The guard sits him down on a chair and then leads the wife to the same room, presumably to check his story. One asylum seeker told me last week that he knew someone who said to the UN officer he had been jailed. The officer asked him where the light switch was in the cell, to the left or the right of the door. He said the switch was on the right. Months later he was told he'd failed because political prisons in Iran do not have light switches.

It is close to noon, Newsha is hungry and we are all restless. Every minute my apprehension increases. I'm tired of staring at the worn-out yellow carpet so I read the pamphlet they've given us. It says every individual has a right to leave his or her country if human rights are violated and to seek asylum in another country, and also that the UNHCR helps refugees to resettle in a third country. But, just as Arya had warned us, on the last page it emphasises that more than ninety-five percent of cases are rejected.

Finally my name is called and I stand up. My knees are stiff. Under my breath I say a prayer my mother taught me when I was seven: 'O God, undo the tie from my tongue and give my heart strength and confidence to utter my words. Make me strong over my enemy.'

I'm taken to interview room 5, a medium-sized room with a desk and two chairs, and a small window suffocated by a thick grey curtain. A middle-aged woman with glasses is sitting behind the desk with a computer in front of her. She indicates to the guard that he should leave us.

'My name is Mersey,' she says. 'I will be interviewing you today. I am originally from France.'

My heart sinks. I'm sure she is the 'French Butcher', the woman I've been told is every asylum seeker's worst nightmare.

'My Farsi interpreter is absent today,' she says. 'We can postpone your interview to another day, or if you can speak even basic English, we can go ahead.'

I cannot tolerate another night of sleeplessness. I want to get this over with. I tell her I used to be a translator in Iran so I know some English, though I don't speak it often.

'Okay then, we should be fine. I am going to begin and if you find it too hard we can stop. Do you have any documentation or identification to show me?' Mersey starts typing and I realise she's going to write down everything we say. She reminds me of Mrs Fotoorchi, my primary school teacher, who had the ability to twist one of your earlobes until you thought it would come off, and then smile and convince you to offer your other ear.

'I do, but the guards took it from me. I have important things in my suitcase but they didn't allow me to bring it in.'

Mersey picks up the phone and in less than two minutes a guard comes in with my suitcase and opens it on the desk. I take my books out, one by one – seven of my best works.

I can see that Mersey is impressed. 'You wrote all these?'

'Yes, ma'am, plus another twelve books I couldn't bring with me.'

Mersey tells the guard to photocopy the cover and the first page of each book for her.

'So you were an author in Iran?' She starts typing again.

'Yes, ma'am. I was a writer and a translator, as well as a doctor. In 1994 I was given an award for the best translator in the country. In fact I would like to say, if you don't mind, that I had a very good life in Iran. I didn't want to leave. By coming to another country I've lost my practice and my recognition as a writer. I'm not using the UN to go to a developed country for financial reasons. I am here because I was in trouble with the intelligence service.'

Mersey nods as she types, and this gives me confidence and hope. 'Tell me about your background in Iran.' She places her fingers expectantly on the keyboard.

So I do. I tell her I was the second child of my Jewish mother, and that my father was a Muslim bus driver. When he married my mother he was forty-two with two other wives and she was only seventeen. My Casanova father first came to see me three weeks after I was born.

I tell her about all the discrimination and oppression I experienced as a Jew, from having to hide my religion to being initially banned from attending university. I tell her that I terminated more than three hundred pregnancies and repaired the virginities of more than a hundred women to save them from so-called honour killings. For doing this I could have been hanged several times over, and I lived in constant fear.

I tell her that in 1994 and 1996 two of my best novels were not allowed to be published. Despite this, I began researching my Jewish heritage in Mashhad for another book, interviewing people with Jewish ancestry and even going to the old abandoned synagogue.

Then in February 1997 I was arrested. After two months of torture my interrogator, Haji Samadi, gave me a chance to be released if I accepted the accusations and became a spy for MOIS. I eventually signed the paper and one evening was released outside town.

I explained how my whole life was totally controlled by Samadi, who was now my handler. I would ring a number using a mobile phone I was given and whenever I called – whatever time of day or night, or even if he was out of town – Samadi would always answer. He began phoning me once every two days, then it was once a day and then twice a day. I was allowed to tell Azita I was working for the government but nothing more.

When Samadi wanted to see me he never arrived at the agreed time and he always came in a different car, so while I waited for him I had to search every passing vehicle. He would never tell me what he or MOIS, which he called 'Tashkilat', were after. One time I might be sent to spy on a Muslim man, and the next a Jew. It took me nine months to realise his organisation was in fact after Jews, and they were sending me to random targets to make sure I couldn't figure out what their real plan was.

I tell her about Mr Sayar, the old photographer who burned my chest with cigarettes after I failed Tashkilat's obedience test. Mersey asks to see the burn marks and when I lift up my shirt, her eyes narrow.

I tell her I come from a country that punishes difference and persecutes pleasure. I tell her I resent my homeland. I'm not proud of a country where ancient glory, ruined monuments and fallen kings are the only things that are celebrated. All I respect is the desert – the barren, burning chest of the land with its thousands of buried stories – and all I miss are the red poppies that bloom after the first rain in spring. Mersey listens carefully and nods.

I tell her I was sent to infiltrate a group of underground dissidents, some Muslim, some Jewish. Because I was a Jew and an author, people respected and trusted me. Jews in Iran know they're under constant surveillance because Tashkilat assumes they're all spies for Israel. My Jewishness made me very valuable to Tashkilat.

After that first test, I turned out to be an excellent spy. But every mission took me deeper into this abyss and I soon realised I knew too much to be left alone, that when Tashkilat no longer needed me I would be eliminated. Each time I left the house to meet Samadi I'd kiss Newsha and say to Azita, 'If I don't come back, just get on with your life and imagine I've been killed in a car accident.' Searching for a victim of Tashkilat could be dangerous.

After a few months of espionage on the dissidents, I was sent to spy on some prominent Jews in Mashhad, and then in Tehran and finally Isfahan. They would invite me to their houses for dinner and say things against the government, words that were sufficient to have them hanged. Tashkilat gave me a sophisticated voice recorder and a special mobile phone that showed our location.

Soon I established a relationship with Saeed, who dedicated his life to making fake passports for Jews who were in trouble and arranging for them to escape. Tashkilat was thirsty for his blood. After I spent weeks working on him he came to rely on me; after all I was a doctor and half of Iran knew my books. He even warned me that I was in danger for writing my book on the history of Iranian Jews.

My heart ached every time I recorded Saeed. I was betraying my own people, people who had children and families and wanted the same things I did: a better Iran with liberty and justice for everyone. I had nightmares constantly – about escaping or dying, or sometimes I'd lead a trembling man to the gallows.

Samadi must have suspected how I felt about what I was doing. He told me he wanted me to turn on the recorder before leaving my car, so he could hear me shutting the door, walking into Saeed's house and saying hello. I said I would; I knew I couldn't fool Tashkilat.

I pause, realising that now is the moment to tell Mersey about the thirteen Jews. This information, I'm certain, will immeasurably strengthen my case. But then I remember my mother's voice begging me to get her out of jail. I think of Newsha and Niloofar waiting for me outside the room, their future happiness dependent on the success of this interview. No matter what I do, someone in my family will suffer. I'm torn to pieces, but I can't let my daughters down.

Mersey is staring at me. I take a deep breath and say, 'Through Saeed I built a bridge to three other Jews who were later arrested and put on death row. There were others . . .'

'Are you talking about the thirteen Jews who were recently imprisoned?' asks Mersey. I can see the surprise in her eyes.

'Yes, ma'am.'

I give her their names. She types my words carefully, then asks me to wait. I can see that she is opening another file on her screen and writing a report there. After fifteen minutes she takes a deep breath, looks at her watch and says, 'Kooshyar, we've been here for four hours. That's enough for today. I want you to come back tomorrow for the rest of the interview.'

I'm startled. This makes no sense. 'But what about my wife? Can she come with me?'

'Of course,' she says. Then for the first time she smiles warmly. 'I know who is telling the truth and who is just wasting my time. Go home and get some rest. I would like to know more about your cooperation with Tashkilat because we've been trying to identify these thirteen Jews and protect them. Your information is really valuable to us.'

I suddenly feel so relieved I want to jump over the desk and hug Mersey. I'm so grateful she's believed me. My heart is full of hope and light.

When I leave the interview room I grab Azita's hand. 'Let's go home. Everything is going to be fine.'

NINE

I sit outside our building, smoking and thinking about the interview. I still have so much to tell Mersey, but I must be brief and to the point. There's no room for error: even though Mersey said she knew I was telling the truth, if I say something that contradicts other facts my case still might be rejected. I have to stay focused and remember dates, times, names. This isn't easy – I was sent to many people over those thirteen months. As I try to recall that period, I find myself drifting away on a new wave of memories from years earlier.

When I was twelve I went to Isfahan for the first time, visiting Jewish relatives with my mother during school holidays. King Abbas I made Isfahan his capital in the sixteenth century, and in the following few decades it turned into one of the world's most lavish, affluent cities. But Abbas was also a brutal ruler who made Iran a Shia state by ruthlessly persecuting Sunni Muslims, which most Persians were at the time. It was one of the most important turning points in Iran's history and that of the Middle East. If it weren't for Abbas, it's likely Shia Islam would have disappeared as a minor branch of the faith.

I felt so excited about meeting my relatives, but they were not particularly kind to me. I could tell by their empty eyes and soulless smiles they did not like me. They thought I was of mixed blood because my father was a Muslim, even though he wasn't a practising one. Still, he was not a Jew so I wasn't pure enough. I could see their resentment, even when they praised me for my high marks at school.

A few days after our arrival I was in the bazaar and fell into conversation with Mr Mostafavi, a sixty-year-old rug seller. He attracted my attention because of the big sapphire ring on his right hand. He was a devout Muslim, though not a zealot, and a lovely soul.

'Your mother was the smartest girl I ever met,' he told me over tea at his shop. 'You should be proud of her. She's worked hard for her life.' He sipped his tea and made himself comfortable on a small timber chair. 'Just before your mother was born her father, Habib, was stabbed to death by fanatical Muslims, right there on that footpath.' He pointed to a narrow cobblestoned lane nearby.

'Your grandmother remarried, to a Jewish man in Tehran, so she moved and sent her three older daughters to Israel. Your mother was adopted by Habib's brother, Abraham.'

I was shocked to hear this. My mother had never really told me much about her parents and any time I asked about them she changed the topic.

'Abraham is a horrible man,' said Mr Mostafavi. 'I'm not saying this because he's a Jew; he is a truly evil individual. He made your mother work at his liquor shop from the age of six. I told him many times to be kind to her but he didn't care. She served alcohol to all sorts of drunk, sleazy men. She was abused often but nobody protected her. She had to work for Abraham, otherwise she would've had no food, no clothes, no education. Later on I found out she was forced to sleep in a small storage room in Abraham's house, while all his children had proper rooms.

'When she was fifteen she met Khalil, the generous, handsome and charismatic bus driver who came to Abraham's shop every now and then. He was twenty-five years older than her but talked very sweetly to her. He told her he was single, that he loved her and would look after her. Your mother was naïve and starving for love, so she believed him and one day she escaped with Khalil to Tehran.'

Mr Mostafavi sighed deeply. 'He took her to his house and told her she was his queen. She was happy for two weeks until one day the door opened and a forty-year-old woman entered with her teenage daughter. The woman's name was Parvin and she was Khalil's second wife. As soon as she found out who your mother was she brutally bashed her. Khalil came home and denied everything, telling Parvin your mother was just a new maid at their house. Your mother was heartbroken and forlorn. She couldn't come back to Isfahan – Abraham would have killed her. After many months of working as a maid at Khalil and Parvin's house, he moved your mother to a basement in Nezam Abad. He told Parvin he'd fired her but he had to get her out because she was pregnant. Your mother also found out Khalil had another wife too, Nahid. She was devastated but had no choice other than to stay.

I sat there stunned by these revelations about my parents. 'When you were eighteen months old, Parvin took you from your mother and threatened to kill her. Your mother became deeply depressed and wanted to commit suicide. She came back to Isfahan as a last resort and my wife looked after her. We talked to her for days, until she started to change her mind and gain her confidence again. Abraham refused to see her but he agreed to send her to Israel. At the last moment your mother decided not to leave you with Parvin. She went back to Tehran but Parvin had set fire to the house to harm you and you were burned badly. You had to spend more than two months in hospital. After you'd recovered, your mother went to the police and they warned Parvin that if she bothered her again she would go to jail.'

As Mr Mostafavi spoke I touched the large scar on the right side of my stomach. I'd known that Parvin had caused it but my mother never told me the full story.

Mr Mostafavi took a deep breath and stared into my eyes. 'Kooshyar, your mother has sacrificed her life for you. Make her proud,' he said.

His words profoundly affected me, and I was deeply touched he'd taken the time to tell me all this. I already respected my mother but now I admired her: for her endurance, her courage and her self-sacrifice. I also now had a better understanding of why her behaviour towards me was sometimes contradictory. Hearing about her dreadful childhood, I realised she'd never felt loved and constantly faced betrayal, neglect and abuse. My mother wanted my brother and me to always be reliant on her, to always want her. This suited Koorosh but I had a greater sense of self-sufficiency. Though

I knew she loved me dearly and was proud of my accomplishments, my mother also resented me for not needing her as my brother did – and so sometimes she would impulsively hurt me. My mother never understood how much I admired her, and she mistook my desire to be independent for careless rebelliousness.

The next morning we arrive at the UN at eight again but this time I'm in Mersey's room less than an hour later. Azita and our daughters are in the waiting room. A whole new group of asylum seekers are being interviewed today, another assembly of despairing humans searching for a glimmer of hope from interrogators who determine their destinies.

I tell Mersey the story of a man I call Mr Ali. He was smart and highly educated, with only a small group of people – university lecturers and authors – in his gatherings. I successfully infiltrated this group and attended five sessions in his house. Soon Mr Ali's right-hand man, Mr Hossein, went missing and two weeks later his decomposing body was found in bush near Mashhad. Some of Mr Ali's other followers were arrested and either jailed for many years or killed. Occasionally Mr Ali himself would go missing and reappear, telling his followers he had been imprisoned and tortured.

Samadi loved my reports about Mr Ali and was intensely interested in his activities. One day, after I gave Samadi information about Mr Ali's recent session with four democracy activists, he said something that indicated he already knew about this secret conversation with the activists. I started to realise that while people who had half Mr Ali's record of dissidence were being given long jail sentences or executed, he was safely practising. It dawned on me then that Mr Ali was a decoy. This was confirmed later when Samadi suddenly told me to forget about Mr Ali and return to Saeed.

Mersey asks me some questions about my cooperation with MOIS and after another hour she seems satisfied. She opens a folder on her desk and goes through some papers.

'Kooshyar, did you ever join a political party in Iran?' she asks.

Suddenly my heart stops. I see she's looking at the support letter faxed by the party's London office.

'No, I didn't,' I tell Mersey.

She stares at me above her spectacles. I've already risked my mother's life once in front of Mersey. I just can't do it again. Besides, if I talk about the monarchist group, I'll also endanger the other members, a horrifying thought after already accidentally giving MOIS the names of three of them. But if I tell Mersey that the fax is fake, as Attaran instructed, my whole case could crumble.

'None at all?' she asks sharply.

I shake my head. 'Not really.'

Mersey closes the folder and leans forward. 'What do you mean?'

'I didn't really act as a member of any political party. That's all I can tell you.'

'But you did take a lot of risks.'

'I know, but not as part of any party.'

'Listen, Kooshyar, you have to be honest with me,' she says. 'So far I have trusted you, and I have information right in front of me showing that you did in fact join a political group, a monarchist party. Is that right?'

She looks at me expectantly. I wish I could tell her that if I say any more my mother will be tortured to death. I return Mersey's intense gaze, willing her to receive my silent message, to see the truth underneath my expression.

I tell her, 'Joining a monarchist party can jeopardise one's vulnerable family members. I can only say that much.'

She nods, and a smile slowly appears across her face. 'I appreciate your difficult situation, Kooshyar.' She takes a deep breath and puts the folder in her drawer. 'Okay, I think I have what I need. As you might be aware, we have to confirm everything with our database and our agents on the ground. This will take time.'

'I understand, ma'am.'

'Now, could you please ask your family to join us?'

'You mean . . .?'

'Yes, I'm not going to double-check your story with your wife.'

I've started to like Mersey. Azita walks into the room with Niloofar in her arms, and Newsha comes over and holds my hand. Mersey gets up from behind her desk and asks Azita if she can hold Niloofar. 'She's gorgeous,' Mersey says, smiling.

'Thank you,' Azita and I reply simultaneously. Then Azita bursts into tears. Mersey hugs her and says, 'You are going to start a new life. Your misery is over.'

These words give us so much hope and courage that we forget about all our troubles in Turkey. When we leave the building, my heart is jumping out of my chest with joy.

Three days after my final interview with Mersey I go to the police headquarters as usual to sign the book. But this time things are different. The Turkish police officer asks my name again, even though he knows it very well after more than ninety days of coming to the same room to sign the same book.

'Kooshyar Karimi from Iran,' I say.

He tells me to wait and leaves the room. I think, What's going on?

Half an hour later he comes back, looking concerned. 'Kooshyar, you have to move,' he says.

'What do you mean?'

'I don't know why but you have to move from here. That's what my boss says.' He speaks in Turkish so I have a bit of trouble following him, but after twenty minutes of broken conversation I realise I have to go to a place called Çankiri, two hours east of Ankara. My involvement in Iranian politics means it's too dangerous to keep me here in Ankara. But are they trying to protect me or the Turkish government? I certainly feel safer in a large metropolis than a small isolated village. Because the UN has probably now notified the government of my knowledge about the thirteen Jews, the Turks are likely to be worried about negative press if any harm were to come to me.

How are we going to cope in a small town? I've been able to create some semblance of normal life by regularly buying things from the stolen goods market in Ulus, such as clothes and even a broken old TV that I managed to fix. I now feel comfortable in our little room three levels under the ground. Finding new accommodation to rent in such a small place will be impossible.

I wait till late at night before I finally tell Azita we have to move. She bursts into tears. I try to calm her down, reminding her that we have to do as we're told and reassuring her we'll soon hear from the UN and be safe in another country. My words are futile.

'I can't do this anymore, I just can't. Do you have any idea how damaged Newsha is? Where are those women you treated in Iran? Who is going to help us now?'

It's a good question. In the morning I contact Bulent.

'What's up, Pislik Yahudi?' That's what he calls me as a joke: 'Dirty Jew'. He's a Muslim but a very moderate one – he drinks alcohol and eats pork. I explain what's happened and he exclaims, 'Çankiri is a shithole!'

'It doesn't matter, Bulent. I have to move there. Can you please help me?'

After a few moments deep in thought he says, 'I don't know anyone in Çankiri and I assume there wouldn't be many places for lease there. Besides, country people are more reluctant to rent to an asylum seeker.'

'I understand,' I mumble in despair.

'How much time do you have?' he asks.

'Ten days.'

'If you pay for my petrol, I can take you there in a couple of days. Hopefully we'll find somewhere and then somehow we'll take your stuff there after that.'

'That sounds like a plan. Thank you so much, Bulent.'

He also reminds me that we have to go to the real estate office and terminate our lease for the current place. I feel nervous. I've been paying my rent on time but I don't know how the real estate agent will react to the news.

At midday on Thursday I walk to the real estate agency. When I enter the old man who dealt with us three months ago is busy doing some paperwork.

'Merhaba!' I say loudly.

'Merhaba abi.' He says hello back to me.

I start trying to explain the situation but he seems upset. The more I talk about the police and their decision, the more confused and annoyed he looks. My Turkish is much better than when I first arrived in the country but I still understand less than fifty percent of the words exchanged in the street. Thankfully Bulent arrives a few minutes later and takes over, talking in fluent Turkish. The old man's expression slowly lightens, and he gets up and walks towards me. I have no idea what he's about to do. He reaches out his hand and we shake. Then he says something that Bulent translates for me.

'You were my best tenant, much better than my Turkish clients. Thank you for always paying your rent on time. God be with you.'

I press his hand and ask Bulent to say to him in Turkish: 'I'm so sorry to break the lease. I'm very grateful for what you did for me and my family.'

After Bulent translates my words the old man pulls me in and hugs me, squeezing me in his big arms. Then he goes back to his desk and writes something on a piece of paper. I look at Bulent and he shrugs his shoulders; he doesn't know what the old man is writing either. Seconds later the old man gets up and gives the paper to Bulent. We leave the office and plan the trip to Çankiri for the next day.

I'm ready at four in the morning for Bulent to pick me up. He turns up soon after with a full tank and we head for Çankiri. As we leave Ankara the houses and streets become narrower and fouler. We drive along a twisted, slender road for two hours until we reach a small village. A rusted sign on the road says in Turkish *Welcome to Çankiri*. It's a town of tiny streets and rickety houses.

It is eight in the morning when we walk into the first real estate agency, a small dank office on the ground floor of a two-storey building. As soon as Bulent says 'asylum seeker', the agent demands that we leave.

There are only five agencies in town. We go to the second and face the same reaction: paranoia and hatred. The person at the third agency tells us we have to wait for the boss, and when he finally appears – hours later – he shakes his head. Bulent is trying to keep me optimistic. I keep thanking him for going through all this hardship and humiliation for us. He says, 'We have to find a roof for Newsha and Niloofar.'

By four in the afternoon we're starving and tired, and almost every store is closing for the day. We rush to a takeaway shop and buy some cheap hamburgers. It is a typical Turkish grocery, selling everything from pliers and power boards to deodorants and condoms, from mousetraps and fly swatters to transistor radios and medicinal herbs. It also has a small kitchen where sandwiches are made. I discuss with Bulent the last real estate office we're going to check and I notice the shopkeeper is listening to us. Eavesdropping is common in small towns like Çankiri.

'Are you looking for a place to rent?' he asks Bulent.

'Yes, for my Iranian friend,' Bulent replies.

The shopkeeper shakes his head. 'Good luck with that.'

'Why is that?' Bulent asks.

'The real estate agent who owns that office hates asylum seekers. Last year he rented a room to an Iranian woman and when she left she didn't give him the final payment. Since then he doesn't even talk to anyone from Iran.' Then he adds, 'We call him Dog. He's a very moody man. His second wife committed suicide three years ago.' He continues chopping tomatoes.

'We really need to find a place for my friend. He's a very good man who pays his rent on time.' Bulent takes out the letter the agent in Ankara gave us and hands it over. The shop owner stops slicing and reads.

When he's finished he says, 'I know about a unit for rent. It's upstairs, right on the top of my shop, and it's got two bedrooms. But the owner is a fussy man.'

'Can you talk to him?' says Bulent. He takes out his driver's licence and student card. 'I'm an English student at Hajetepe University and I live in Ankara. I can be the guarantor. In fact I'll sign the lease, so if he gets behind in his rent I'll be accountable and will pay it. Is that good enough?'

'Maybe. I'll let you know by tomorrow.'

Bulent gives the shop owner, whose name is Barish, his mobile number and we head for the last real estate office. The man behind the desk is a fat, bald middle-aged Turk with a thick moustache. He looks up from his newspaper and says, 'How can I help you?'

'My name is Bulent, I'm from Ankara and I need a unit for rent. Doesn't really matter what part of Çankiri, just a place to live for three to six months.'

The Turkish man looks at me suspiciously. 'Is it for you?' he asks Bulent.

Bulent hesitates. 'No, it's for my friend Kooshyar. He is a doctor from Iran. He's waiting for his visa to go to —'

'No. I have nothing to rent to evsizs.' He stands up, puts his newspaper on the desk and waves for us to get out.

'But I can guarantee him. And here's a letter from his previous real estate agent.' Bulent tries to show the piece of paper to the man but he pushes us out of his office.

'I said no!'

At seven in the evening we arrive back in Ankara empty-handed and extremely disappointed. I have no idea how I'm going to face Azita.

'Don't worry, Kooshyar,' says Bulent. 'There's still that unit above the grocery shop.'

'I know, but our chances are next to nothing.'

'You never know. Besides, you're one lucky bastard!' Though he's trying to make me laugh, I'm finding it hard to smile.

On the way to our basement I think about how the Çankiri real estate agents behaved towards me. I was treated like a terrorist. Although maybe they have a point, considering Iran's support of Islamic terrorists in the last three decades. I can't blame the Turks for being suspicious.

'So what happened?' Azita asks later in the evening, once the girls are asleep. Newsha has been very down – she constantly talks about Iran and wants to go back. Her arm is still in a sling and she's in pain every day. It breaks my heart that when we go to the small park near home, she can't play on anything.

'Did you find a place to rent? And is it a nice town? Does it have a park for the kids?' Azita asks.

'Yes, it's a beautiful little place, with lots of greenery, and the people are friendly.' I know she won't come if I tell her the truth.

'But you didn't answer the question. Did you find a place?'

'Yes, yes, I did. Thank God for Bulent.' Another lie.

'What is it? A unit?'

'Yes, it's a unit. There weren't many places available, of course, because it's a small town, but we found somewhere.'

'Did you sign the lease? We only have a week or so to move.'

'Yes but we have to wait for the landlord to approve it. It's not that easy.'

Azita looks into my eyes. 'Are you sure you've found a place?' she asks suspiciously.

'Yes. In a day or two we'll get the confirmation and then we can move there.'

The next day there's no news from Bulent. The following day I wait until midday and call him. He says he hasn't heard anything from the landlord, so I beg him to contact Barish to find out what's happening. Bulent rings me back an hour later. 'The landlord wants to meet you.'

'What does that mean?'

'I think he wants to see if you're trustworthy before renting it out to you.'

'But Bulent, I can't go by myself. It'll be pointless because of my Turkish. Please come with me.' I know I'm asking too much but I'm desperate.

'Okay. I have exams tomorrow and the next day. We can go there next Wednesday, but you'll have to pay for my petrol again.'

'Of course, that's fine.' Petrol is expensive in Turkey and I only have nine hundred dollars left, but we simply have to find a place to live.

When we arrive back in Çankiri the following Wednesday, we go straight to the grocery shop. I notice it's on the outskirts of town, technically in the last block: beyond there's nothing but bare land. Opposite the building is a small river that runs through the main part of the town.

When we get to the shop, before we can ask about the landlord, Barish says, 'I have an Iranian customer who's been living here for almost two years. I told him your story and he's keen to share his accommodation.'

'That's great. Can we meet him?' I ask enthusiastically.

'Let me give him a call.'

Shortly afterwards a man in his late forties appears in the doorway and introduces himself as Hamed. He's delighted another Iranian will be living here and we speak Farsi to each other – an immense relief.

'Are you an asylum seeker?' Hamed asks me.

'Yes, just had my interview with UNHCR.'

'Fucking bastards. I had an interview four years ago. I was rejected, like so many others, and have been waiting for them to reopen my file. I've even forgotten what my house in Iran looks like. It took me six months to find a place here. People are so hostile to refugees – small-town mentality.'

Hamed's manner and turn of phrase suggests he's highly educated, so I ask about his background. 'I was a university chemistry lecturer,' he tells me. 'Now look at me. They treat me like garbage.'

I nod in sympathy and he says, 'Where I'm living is far from perfect but there's space for other people. If you like I can show it to you. The landlord is a nice man – there aren't many of them round here.'

'Yes please, I'm more than happy to see it. I'm not fussy.'

Bulent and I follow Hamed through the narrow streets of Çankiri. After twenty minutes Hamed stops at a small ancient wooden door. He kicks it open and we walk through a cobblestoned yard towards an old mudbrick building with a large shed next to it. We enter the shed, which has a thatched roof, bricks walls, and stinks of sheep and cow droppings, and I realise it's actually a stable. Hamed has placed his blankets and pillows in a corner and there are some pots next to a small woodfired stove.

'This is it,' Hamed says. 'What do you think? There's probably room for another three or four people.'

I'm speechless. I look at Bulent, who's also in shock. I wonder, How can I tell Newsha this is her new home? How would I convince Azita to move into a stable?

Hamed says, 'I'm paying ten dollars a week. You'd only have to pay half.'

Bulent gently says, 'Brother, thank you so much for your help. We'll think about it and let you know.'

'Okay. All the best with your search, but I know this town very well. People won't rent to you even if you're rich, just because you're Iranian. And don't forget you're an asylum seeker!'

On our way back to the grocery shop I try hard not to cry. The thought of my daughters living in a stable cuts through my heart. Bulent pats me on the shoulder and says, 'Don't lose hope, Pislik Yahudi.'

When we arrive, Barish has some news. 'I spoke to the landlord and he's finally agreed to see you here at five-thirty,' he says to Bulent. I look at the time: it's now three-thirty.

'Go for a walk around town in the meantime. By the way, the landlord is a very strict Muslim. He won't even shake your hand if you've used aftershave, as it has alcohol in it.'

As we leave the shop I wonder whether the landlord will shoot me if he finds out I'm a Jew. Thank God I'm not wearing aftershave; the last time I cared about such a thing was more than six months ago. But I'm also worried about Bulent. He should be at home with his fiancée and I feel so uncomfortable, making him go through all this for me.

'I don't know how to thank you, Bulent, but I hope I'll be a free man soon and return the favour,' I say to him.

'Don't worry, Kooshyar. Let's just pray this man agrees to rent out his unit to you.'

We walk along the river towards the centre of town. Almost every building in Çankiri has three or four storeys. Most people in Turkey live in units, including Bulent and his mother. With the country's overpopulation, struggling economy and high unemployment, there aren't many who can afford to live in an actual house.

We come across a couple of women with baskets, selling tiny fish caught from the river. They're so small that I wonder out loud who would eat them. 'People mince them, including their bones and guts, then fry them and eat them with a piece of bread,' Bulent explains.

We're ten minutes early when we return to the grocery shop. Barish is serving customers and selling eggs, homegrown tomatoes and onions. The most common foods here are eggs, green beans and bread. Most Turkish families, especially in the country, can only afford to buy meat once or twice a week.

Time passes slowly. It will be dark soon and we'll have to head back to Ankara. When the landlord is fifteen minutes late Bulent politely asks whether he's forgotten his appointment with us.

Barish just shakes his head. 'He will come.'

After another half an hour there's still no sign of him. At six-thirty Bulent finally loses patience. 'We have to go back soon. Could you please give him a call?'

Barish looks at his watch and after serving a customer he takes out his mobile phone and calls the landlord.

'No, they're still here. I see . . . Okay.' He hangs up then says to us, 'He can't come today. He has a visitor.'

'You must be kidding,' says Bulent. 'We've driven all the way up from Ankara and we've been waiting for hours, and now he says he can't see us for just a few minutes? This is ridiculous!'

'Listen, I'm not a real estate agent. I just wanted to help you and now there's nothing else I can do for you. Please leave,' says Barish.

We walk out, me trailing behind Bulent. It's getting dark already. Bulent is silent. Suddenly I have an idea, and start turning back.

'Where are you going, Kooshyar?' calls Bulent.

When I re-enter the shop, Barish is serving a customer and gives me a furious look. I wait for him to finish then ask for the landlord's address.

'No, I can't give it to you.' He walks over to the other side of his shop. I follow him.

'Brother, please, I just need to talk to him.'

Barish shakes his head and avoids my eyes.

'I have two little daughters, and my youngest is only a baby. For God's sake, please help me.'

Bulent walks in. Barish points at me and says to him, 'Tell your friend I'm not going to give him the landlord's address.'

'Would you trust me with it? I promise I won't tell the landlord how we got it,' says Bulent. He then says something in Turkish, and I can see that something's changed. Barish looks at me, takes out a piece of paper and writes down the address, then gives it to Bulent.

We walk the streets of Çankiri asking passers-by for directions. The landlord's name is Habib and luckily one of the people we come across knows him very well. 'You have to go to the other side of town. Continue straight and at the end of this road, turn left and keep going until you reach the roundabout, then turn right and continue on until you see the sign for Gholamoglu supermarket.

Just opposite that there's a big new two-storey house with white bricks and a black roof. That's Habib's house.'

Bulent thanks the man who, while we're walking away, giggles and says, 'Habib won't like a visitor with a ponytail.' Now I have to worry not only about Bulent's aftershave, but also about his modern clothes and long hair. Turkey is slowly westernising but I can see there's significant resistance, especially among the older generation.

In less than half an hour we're standing in front of a magnificent house. Bulent looks at me nervously. 'It's almost seven o'clock. I don't think it's a good idea to knock on his door.'

I lean forward and press the doorbell. A musical sound echoes inside the building, then there's silence. Bulent takes a step back, as if he's going to be attacked by a python.

'Who is it?' It's a young voice.

'Bulent Kaya.'

A boy in his early teens opens the door. Bulent asks, 'Is this Habib's house?'

'That's my father,' says the boy.

'Can you call him, please?'

We wait restlessly in the dark street. If Habib refuses me, my family will have to sleep in the streets of Çankiri. Eventually a large man in his late forties appears at the door. He's wearing a white shirt and holds prayer beads in his hand.

'Salam-al-alaykom,' he says seriously, looking us up and down. He doesn't say the modern word 'Merhaba', but instead uses the old-fashioned Islamic greeting in Arabic.

'Alaykom-al-salam,' we reply.

Bulent says, 'Mr Habib, I am sorry to bother you at such an odd time of night. My friend Kooshyar is an Iranian asylum seeker and he has to live in Çankiri for the next few months. We were wondering if you would be kind enough to rent your unit to him.'

Habib turns his severe gaze from Bulent's ponytail to me. He looks unhappy. Before he says anything a little girl, around three years old, runs up to him and grabs his feet. Habib pats her hair and murmurs, 'Go back inside, Niloofar.' She skips away.

Habib turns back to us and asks sarcastically, 'You want to rent my unit? For this Irani stranger?'

'Yes, sir,' Bulent murmurs.

Habib takes a deep breath and says, 'But he is from Iran and you are one of us. What makes you come and ask me this? How do you know he'll pay his rent?' He stares at Bulent.

'Because for the last three months he has been paying it in Ankara.'

'But how do you know he will keep paying it? Obviously he won't have a job here.'

Bulent is quiet for a moment. Then he says, 'The Prophet Mohammad tells us to treat our guests as our brothers. This man has come to our country with no hope and no shelter. I see it as my duty to help my Muslim brother.'

Habib's face softens slightly. 'You have horrible hair, Bulent, but also a great heart,' he says. 'I'm sorry, though – that unit is not for rent, and this Irani man is not a guest in my house so I am not responsible for him.'

Habib reaches for the door and starts to shut it. I feel like I'm drowning in a vast ocean and this is the last stick floating on the water.

'Mr Habib, please look at this before you close the door.' I pull out of my pocket my small picture of Niloofar and show it to him.

The photograph was taken a few days ago by Bulent's fiancée, and shows Niloofar sitting on the concrete floor of the basement with nothing around her, looking lost and lonely. 'She has the same name as your daughter. She's only five months old.'

Habib looks at the picture for a while and then gives it back to me. 'She is cute.'

There is silence again. With my heart pounding I say, 'Mr Habib, you are my last hope. I have searched everywhere in Çankiri but no one wants to give his house to an evsiz.' I look directly into his eyes.

He is quiet. I cannot guess what's going on in his religious mind. However, I have learned one thing in my life: we humans have much more than religion to unite us.

'What's your name?' he asks.

'Kooshyar Karimi.'

'Come inside, Kooshyar,' he says, before walking off.

Bulent and I look at each other. 'Come in, yallah!' calls Habib from somewhere within the house.

We enter and follow Habib's voice to a vast living area, decorated with three sets of luxury furniture in different colours and styles.

'Please have a seat,' says Habib, sitting down in the largest chair. 'Have you had dinner?' His tone is friendly for the first time.

'Yes, we're fine,' says Bulent, though we're actually starving.

'Get us some tea, Ebro!' Habib calls out to his wife. A minute or so later Ebro, a good-looking young woman with a scarf carefully covering her hair, appears with a tray of tea. After our exhausting day, the tea tastes wonderful.

'How many children do you have, Kooshyar?' asks Habib.

'Two, sir. Niloofar and Newsha, who is five years old.'

'Allah bless them,' says Habib.

'Mr Habib, Kooshyar pays his rent on time, I promise,' says Bulent.

'My unit is not for rent, Bulent. I don't need money from that place – thanks to Allah I am rich enough not to rely on that.'

'But we were told that it is,' Bulent insists.

'Last year my mother-in-law passed away. She was a great woman, with strong faith in Allah. Before she died she asked me to do something for the poor, so I decided to give that place to a family who are really desperate for shelter. So many have tried to convince me they deserve it. Even though they were poor and desperate, I didn't feel any of them were right for my mother-in-law's last wish. Until tonight you, ponytail man, brought this Irani to me.'

I am stunned. Suddenly I have enormous respect for Habib. He turns to me and says, 'It's a nice unit, with three rooms, but it's a bit hard to keep warm in winter.'

He asks Ebro to bring him the keys. While we wait for her to come back, I close my eyes and silently pray to Adonai.

'Here, Kooshyar, these are the keys to the unit. You can move in any time.' I have tears in my eyes. I don't know what to say. I glance at Bulent, who looks dumbfounded. 'Take the keys and go back to Ankara. Your children must be waiting for you.'

'But what about the ren—' Bulent elbows me in the chest.

Habib says with a smile, 'Go and tell the news to your family. Bring your Niloofar to Çankiri – we will look after her.'

As we walk back to the car, Bulent turns to me and says, 'You Pislik Yahudi, you definitely have an angel looking after you.'

TEN

It is 2 October 1999. We're leaving almost everything I've collected over the last three months in Ankara and are starting afresh. I know there's nowhere in Çankiri that sells cheap stolen items, but I'm sure we'll find a way to survive. We take two suitcases, packed with children's clothes and bits and pieces, as well as the blankets and pillows Bulent's mother gave us.

'Where are we going, Baba?' asks Newsha.

'To a beautiful town called Çankiri and we're going to live next to a gorgeous river for a while.'

She looks at me blankly. I can see the dark circles under her beautiful eyes, like those under Niloofar's and Azita's and my own. These shadows are beacons of loneliness and neglect, of hopelessness and misery. They reveal the true depth of our sorrow and despair.

'Look after yourself,' says Bulent, shaking my hand. Saying goodbye to him and Funda is awful – I don't know if we'll see them again.

I hug him and say, 'I owe you big-time, brother.'

Funda and Azita are hugging and crying loudly. Just before I get on the bus Bulent reaches into his pocket. He grabs my hand and pushes something into it, closing my fist around it.

'I want you to have this – it will protect you.'

I can feel that it's made of metal but have no idea what it is. I suspect it's expensive. 'But why, Bulent?'

'Because you changed my life. Now, put it in your pocket and don't look at it until you get to Çankiri.'

I do as he says and walk onto the bus after Azita and Newsha, holding Niloofar in my arms. Before I sit down I see Bulent still standing there.

'I'll miss you, you crazy bastard!' I yell out.

'I'll miss you, Pislik Yahudi!' he replies.

The trip in the packed, stuffy bus is bumpy and tiring. When we finally reach Çankiri it's a cold, cloudy and gloomy evening. We walk for forty-five minutes from the bus terminal to the unit. I've only seen it from the outside so I'm nervous about what we will find. When we get to the grocery shop, Barish is there.

'Merhaba, Kooshyar!' he yells out as we enter. 'Did he rent it out to you?' I nod proudly and we walk through to the narrow staircase that leads to the apartments above.

'Baba, our new house is above the ground,' says Newsha excitedly.

The building has nine units on four levels. We are on level two, right above Barish's shop. When we open the door we gasp with joy: it has large windows and we can see the world outside, even though the view is only of a few leafless trees and a thin trickle of water called the Çankiri River.

That night we lay out the blankets and our spare clothes on the concrete floor for makeshift beds. Azita and the children fall asleep as soon as their heads hit the pillows, but as usual my thoughts keep me awake. I have no idea how long we'll have to stay here, or how long Habib will let us live in this unit, or what is awaiting us at the end of this journey.

I get up and go over to the window. There's a full moon and I can see the streak of water across the road. I take the gift from Bulent out of my pocket. It's a chain with a Star of David hanging from it. I squeeze it in my hands. I remember carving a Star of David on the wall of our basement apartment with a rusty nail when I was six years old. That star became a constant source of hope and relief for me, and I took an oath on it to always keep my devotion and to help others. I place Bulent's gift around my neck, look at the moon and take my oath again, knowing that while we're in Turkey I'll have to keep the necklace hidden. And so our life in Çankiri begins.

Our first task the next morning is to register as asylum seekers. The police station is in the centre of town and it takes us forty-five minutes to get there. While we're registering, a short-tempered officer with a name badge saying *Sergeant Yashar Ibtehal* tells me I have to sign twice a day, morning and afternoon.

'But in Ankara it was just once a day,' I tell him.

'I have special orders for your case. Twice a day – is that clear?'

Then we go for a walk and find the bazaar. We also pass a decent-sized supermarket, near the town's main roundabout, as well as many small grocery shops. We also come across a small green patch with a rusted slide and an old swing. This is Çankiri Park. It's now early afternoon and we're tired and want to go home, but Newsha insists on trying the swing. There's a Turkish boy on it, his mother pushing him. After almost twenty minutes they're still there, giggling as they watch us waiting. Finally Newsha goes forward and, surprisingly, says confidently in Turkish, 'My turn.'

'Get lost,' says the boy, and his mother laughs. It breaks my heart and I pull Newsha aside. I need to distract her. I see an ice-cream booth near the park.

'Look, Newsha, ice-cream!'

'But we can't afford it,' Azita murmurs in my ear. I don't care. For ten cents I buy Newsha a cone with one scoop of homemade ice-cream. She's happy again and we walk back home.

Over the next few days, life returns to some sort of routine but we're extremely lonely. We've heard nothing from Arya and Shadi since their mysterious disappearance, and I just hope they're all right. On Friday there's a temporary market in the centre of town and we browse through it. Though everything is cheaper than in Ankara, it's still too expensive for us. We buy some of the tiny fish from the river and Azita cooks them with olive oil and green beans. Newsha hates them and eats bread and cheese instead; Azita and I force down a few mouthfuls with water, and vomit all through the night. It takes us three days to feel normal again.

One morning on my way to the police station, I see ash raining from the sky and there's a strong smell of smoke in the air. Soon my shirt is covered with slag and I can hardly see the street in front of me. When I reach the station the same angry officer is there, resting his legs on his desk and reading a newspaper. He throws the pen at me without saying anything. As a sergeant he should love asylum seekers – we behave better than anybody else, because we know we'll be deported if we do anything wrong.

I try to sign the book but the pen isn't working.

'Sergeant Yashar, I'm sorry but I need another pen,' I mumble.

'Who said you can call me by my first name? I am Officer Ibtehal! Got it?'

'Yes, sir.'

I shake the pen but it's out of ink, and I'm too scared to tell him again. I stand there like a statue.

Eventually Officer Ibtehal notices me. 'Signed?'

'Sir, the pen is out of ink.'

'So? Go get a pen, then. This is a police station, not a stationery shop.' I can see he's doing a crossword, pen in hand.

I walk out and, after searching for a while, find a small shop and buy a pen for fifteen cents. When I return to the station, Officer Ibtehal is still holding his pen.

I sign and write the date and time in the book. Before I leave he glances at his newspaper and says, 'Plenty of oil in Iran, yeah?'

'Yes, Sergeant.'

'Bastard.' Somehow it's my fault Iran owns cheap energy. Then I realise the ash and smoke are from burning firewood. Heating is expensive in Turkey, and it's already colder here than anything I experienced in Iran. I'm relieved we brought Bulent's mother's blankets.

Time passes slowly in Çankiri. The nights are deeply disheartening. Azita and I talk about our future and I always end up saying that if our case is rejected she can take the kids back to Iran. Then Azita cries and I try to calm her down by pointing out that

Mersey seemed positive we'd be successful. Eventually Azita falls asleep and I stay awake, until two or three in the morning, thinking.

To keep my mind occupied I'm translating a book Bulent gave me about the constellations and calendars of the ancient Aryans, specifically in the Persian Empire. It contains remarkable research that shows ancient Persian palaces did not follow Assyrian architecture, as previously thought, but instead were designed according to their own mythology based on astronomical observations. I have always loved translating such books, and working on this one is a welcome distraction. Whenever I feel exhausted from translating, I work on a novel I'm writing about people who betray each other.

One day, not long after moving to Çankiri, we're returning from the police station when we decide to go to the park so Newsha can play. As we walk towards it we can see there are no other children around – Newsha will finally get to play on the swing. After a while another family arrives, with two boys around ten and twelve years old. Azita pulls my sleeve. 'I bet they're Iranian.'

One of the boys goes over to Newsha and says something in Farsi. She's so excited she runs up to me with a wide smile. 'Baba, this is Neema. He's my friend.'

Soon Azita and I are chatting with his parents. Finding people who speak our language is like discovering water in the middle of a scorching desert. We can see that Asef and his wife Soosan are delighted too.

'Çankiri is where the Turkish police send political asylum seekers – not many end up here,' says Asef. 'You must have a dangerous case.'

'Yes.' I can't tell him any details of my story.

'How long have you been here?' Soosan asks us.

'Only ten days or so but it feels like a century,' says Azita, sighing.

'We've been here for more than a year and we still haven't heard anything about our interview,' says Soosan. My heart sinks.

When the kids finish playing we head home. The boys are curious about Newsha's cast and want to know why her right arm is in a sling. Not mentioning the Turkish boy who pushed her, Newsha tells them she slipped off a swing in Ankara and broke her arm.

As soon as we walk past the ice-cream booth Newsha, Neema and his brother, Navid, ask for some. Asef and I glance at each other.

'Tomorrow, I promise,' I say to Newsha.

'If you behave tonight, you can have a cone tomorrow,' Asef says. And we speed up our pace.

A small Turkish girl comes towards us, holding her mother's hand and licking strawberry ice-cream. I watch Newsha stare at her as she walks past. I enclose my daughter's small hand in mine and look away.

The next morning, a Friday, I meet Asef accidentally at the police station. This time the officer behind the desk is a junior policeman who's not as revolting as Officer Ibtehal, maybe because he hasn't been poisoned by bribery and anger yet.

'No fax for you, Asef,' says the young officer. Asef shakes his head in disappointment.

After signing the book, Asef and I leave and continue talking. He says, 'I feel guilty that because of my activities in Iran, our kids are here with no education and no future.'

I know exactly how he feels. 'So you can't go back to Iran?' I ask him.

'Are you kidding? They'd cut me to pieces.'

We walk in silence for a while. When we get to the ice-cream booth I ask, 'So, how do you know if the UN has decided the result of your interview?'

'They send a fax to the police station. That's why whenever I go to sign the book I ask if there's a fax for me. The police know me very well by now, although that's also because the only other Iranian asylum seeker here is Hamed. I feel sorry for him – I think he's about to lose it.'

'I know. I met him when I was looking for a place to rent,' I say. Remembering Hamed's stable makes me feel grateful once more for Habib's generosity.

We keep talking until we reach the main road out of town. Asef lives in a very small one-bedroom unit across the road from me on the other side of the river.

'We should catch up some time for a cup of tea,' says Asef.

'That would be great.'

It's not long before our families are meeting almost every second night. I find Asef a pleasant man – he's in his late forties, was a qualified engineer in Iran, and is quite knowledgeable and humble. Though we become close, and we talk constantly about our interviews, we don't confide in each other our reasons for seeking asylum.

One night we're walking back from Asef's unit, around midnight, and I'm carrying Niloofar while Azita holds Newsha's hand. We hear wild dogs barking and shake with fear – these diseased dogs can kill. We speed up but after we've crossed the narrow, rotting bridge I notice a pile of wood in front of an old house. It looks as if builders have left it behind after finishing some renovations. I head over to have a look.

'Come on, Kooshyar, let's go. The dogs are going to get us,' Azita whispers loudly. I check the woodpile: there are five long logs, wet and mouldy from the rain. I form a plan and decide to return later.

The next day I deal with a more pressing concern: taking off Newsha's cast. I cut it with a serrated knife, which takes hours. Newsha is brave but I can see she's trying to hide the pain, and I feel pride mixed with anxiety.

While removing the cast I try to remember how her fracture looked on the X-ray. Though children's bones tend to mend very well, I'm worried her arm has healed crookedly or that she might have some permanent nerve damage. We can't afford another X-ray or a proper examination by a paediatric orthopaedic surgeon.

'It's sore, Baba,' she says, trying to move her arm.

I teach Newsha an exercise to mobilise her arm, and over the next few weeks Azita and I encourage her to perform it regularly. At first she often cries in pain but after two weeks she has almost restored normal function and can play with Neema and Navid.

On a cold morning a few days after removing Newsha's cast I decide to sneak out and pick up the logs we saw on our way home from Asef and Soosan's. I can't imagine that anyone else would want these soggy, mouldy lumps of wood. The logs are heavy and I struggle to carry them home, eventually resorting to dragging them behind me. I have even greater difficulty getting them through the building's front door and up the staircase to the second level. At least I don't have to go through the grocery shop to get to the stairs, which have a separate entrance. When I finally drop the wood on the floor of the unit, Azita wakes up.

'Have you lost your mind?'

'I'm going to make a table for us,' I announce, as proud as the architect of the Empire State Building.

With tools I've borrowed from Barish I start sawing and hammering and sanding and chiselling. I also pull out the crooked, rusty nails so they can be reused. Straightening nails was the first job I ever had, when I was a cobbler at the age of five. As I work I have an unusual, bitter taste in my mouth, which I attribute to the effort of dragging the logs so far. Finally, at six in the evening, I've finished. It's the ugliest table in Turkey and would require four men to lift it.

'Are you okay, Kooshyar? You look so pale,' says Azita.

'I'm fine. A bit tired, that's all,' I murmur, wiping the sweat from my face.

Less than half an hour later I'm feverish, perspiring profusely and shaking violently. I feel disoriented and unaware of what's going on around me. Later on, in a lucid moment, I realise I've contracted a severe case of influenza, and I know that more people die from that than from AIDS.

Azita is terrified. Every day Soosan brings a bowl of soup with chickpeas and noodles but I can't eat anything.

'Please try, Kooshyar,' says Azita. 'You were hallucinating last night. You kept shouting, "Get out! Run away! Run!"'

On the second night of my illness there's a knock on the door. Azita opens it and Officer Ibtehal walks in. 'Where is Kooshyar?' he demands.

'He's sick,' Azita says nervously.

He comes to my room and sees me in bed. As he towers over me I try to look directly at him but my vision's blurry. I feel as if I've swallowed razor blades. 'Hello, Officer,' I manage to whisper.

'You didn't come to the station today.'

'He is sick, Officer. Very sick,' says Azita.

'Are you sure you haven't been out of Çankiri?' Officer Ibtehal asks me.

'I really . . . can't . . .'

'Then I'll send someone to make sure you haven't left town until you're well again. Okay?'

'Okay,' I say weakly before passing out.

An hour later I wake up with Azita's voice in my ear, begging me to see a doctor. But I say no – we can't afford it. On the third night I have a seizure.

'Wake up, Kooshyar! Wake up!' She shakes me vigorously. 'You had a fit. We must take you to hospital.'

I refuse, though I wonder if I've developed viral meningitis. I go back into a stupor.

For five more days my whole body aches as if I've been hit by a truck. However, eventually my energy begins to return and a few days later I'm back on my feet again. The first time Officer Ibtehal sees me in the station again he says sarcastically, 'Evsiz, you don't die so easily.' I sign the book and leave the room, demeaned and hurt. I ask myself, How is it that some people are simply incapable of kindness?

On my way home I remember a fiery speech given by the mullah in our slum encouraging us to join the war against Iraq. Mullah Mohamad was a bald, squint-eyed 75-year-old with a long white beard who looked like one of Snow White's dwarfs. He was connected to everybody in the slum, if not by blood then through marriage or the influence of money. His sparkling altruism was ostensibly for the glory of Allah, but in reality it was merely camouflaged egoism spiced with dogmatic ideology. The mullah would respond to any question by quoting or paraphrasing the Koran. At least he had a talent for making his rehearsed phrases sound spontaneous and original.

When Mullah Mohamad gave the speech about the war, I was fourteen and the conflict had been going for four years. In a packed mosque I sat next to my friend Vahid. Because we were now taller than an AK-47, in the eyes of the mullah we should've been battling infidels instead of going to school or playing football in the streets.

Mullah Mohamad said, 'I wish I was younger so I could be at the front line. One shouldn't rest at night in bed while our brave men are fighting to protect our Islamic territory with their lives.'

Vahid elbowed me. 'Why is his son Hassan not at war?'

'He's a wuss,' I replied. 'I scratched his face with dry toast at school one day and he ran to the principal.' We both giggled.

The mullah passionately urged us to follow the path of Imam Ali, the most important figure in Shia Islam after Mohammad. 'Nobody could defeat him in battle. He had the power of ten men!'

'Then how come eleven men didn't get together and bash him up?' I whispered to Vahid.

The mullah warned the crowd, 'Saddam is secretly supported by Israel. In fact all the troubles in the Middle East, such as war, corruption and poverty, are caused by Jews.'

I wondered, If the six million Jews in Israel can cause so much trouble for the hundreds of millions of Muslims in the Middle East, they must be very clever.

Then the mullah raised his voice even more. 'Allah says in the Holy Koran that every man who dies fighting for Islam will go to heaven straight away and be given seventy beautiful virgins.'

There have been hundreds of thousands of martyrs in Iran. Every street, every important building or square or lane has been named after one. Islamic fatalism has destined young Iranians to a paradise that resembles a chaotic, overcrowded brothel.

After Mullah Mohamad eventually finished his invitation to violence and murder, he sat down behind a small desk in a corner of the mosque, opened a big book and started writing the names of volunteers for the war. Several young boys and men lined up, while some old men enjoyed tea and biscuits as they relaxed on the massive handwoven carpet. Mullah Mohamad offered advice to each volunteer, and his favourite line seemed to be: 'When you look into the mirror, see who is in there, not whom you want to see in there that is not you.' Nobody knew what he meant, probably including the mullah himself.

A young Revolutionary Guard started loudly lamenting Imam Hossein's death, a tragedy that took place almost fourteen hundred years ago, and many joined him in his weeping. Sorrow is my nation's delight. We can't be detached from it, like the interlocking fingers of two hands. In a land where freedom and joy are forbidden, grief and malice are admired.

That night after dinner I said to my mother, 'I know Dad has three wives, but can a man sleep with more women?'

My mother glared at me. 'What do you mean?'

'I mean, can a man sleep next to a few women in one night?'

'How many women?'

'Seventy?'

My mother took off her rubber slipper and ran after me.

ELEVEN

'I'm going to Ankara tomorrow,' says Asef, when he visits us with his family one evening.

'Why?' I ask him.

'To see if I can catch my case officer leaving the UN building so I can remind him I'm still waiting for my result. I do it every two or three months.'

'But that makes no sense.'

'I know.' He shakes his head. 'But what else can you do? I've heard that some people have spoken to their case officers outside.'

'That's a myth, Asef. I've heard a lot of bullshit from asylum seekers, like you can bribe the case officers or get a lawyer to defend you. You should know by now that these are fabrications.'

'But I'm going crazy waiting. I need to do something.'

'Have you even seen your case officer once since you've been doing this?'

'No. I think they leave through a back door. But I'll try again tomorrow. I'm hoping that if he comes out to the street, I can jolt his memory.'

'But he probably wouldn't remember you. They interview people every day.'

'I know, Kooshyar, I know.' He stares at the ground.

'I'm sorry,' I say. 'I just don't want you to be disappointed.'

'No, I understand. But you'll see – there comes a point when you want to do something other than just endlessly wait.'

'But how do you get around the police? We're not allowed to leave town.'

'I go at six in the morning and sign, then catch a bus to Ankara and stay outside the UN building for the whole day. Around six at night I get on the bus for Çankiri and sign the police book at eight-thirty.'

'But if they find out you'll be deported.'

'I know, Kooshyar, but I have to go. It's my only hope.'

'Just be careful. Please,' I say to him, and he nods.

Asef goes to Ankara and comes back with no result. He's frustrated but at least the police didn't find out he left Çankiri.

Time passes slowly. When I go to the police station every day I try to ask about a fax but before I've opened my mouth they tell me there isn't one.

I begin to understand how Asef has got to the point where he'll risk everything to go to Ankara. He wants to feel like he has some control over his life. Hanging on for news feels like waiting to die in the bottom of a deep, dark well. But I worry that before long I too will break the rules and jeopardise our future.

Asef and I begin to look out for each other. I still have the mobile phone I purchased in Ulus but there's now only two dollars' credit on it, so I only keep it in case of an emergency or if Bulent needs to contact me. However, after my influenza, Asef and I use it to check on each other on nights we don't see each other. Before going to bed I ring his mobile, let it ring twice then hang up. I like to think of it as saying to him, 'I'm fine, brother. How are you?' When Asef responds with two rings of his own, he's saying, 'I'm fine, brother. Good night.'

It is already bitterly cold in Çankiri. I'm worried the children will get sick when winter arrives. Only two groups in Turkey can heat their houses with electricity: the super-rich, and the crooks. And I am not super-rich.

I walk around Çankiri for three days until I find a broken toaster, thrown out by its previous owner. I bring it home and take out the heating element, which I wrap around a big brick and attach to the power point. Now I need power. I wait until midnight and go into the corridor. There are three units next to each other on this level. Azita is with me to let me know if anyone starts coming.

'Kooshyar, are you sure this is the right thing to do?' says Azita.

'Of course not. It's stealing.'

I place a chair outside our unit door and stand on it, reaching into the meter that controls our electricity supply. After gently breaking the lead case, I open the glass door and use a screwdriver to stop the counter.

'Done,' I say with a big smile on my face, as if I've dismantled a bomb in a packed football stadium.

We go back inside and I turn on our new heater. It's surprisingly effective as long as you stay next to it. Azita and I move the girls so they're closer to it and we all sleep soundly that night, although at four in the morning I turn it off and reconnect the meter. I know I'm breaking the law but I can't let Newsha and Niloofar freeze to death.

The next day, on our way back from the police station, we walk past a man who looks familiar. He says hello in Farsi and keeps going.

'Who is he?' asks Azita.

Suddenly I remember – it was Hamed. He's lost so much weight I didn't recognise him. 'He's an asylum seeker. He's been here four years, waiting for UNHCR to help him.'

'Oh no,' says Azita. When we get home she starts crying. Hamed's plight has underlined our situation, and she cannot bear it. I understand her frustration, and want to do something.

But what? It's now more than a month since my interview with the UN. I hardly sleep; I'm losing my patience and my sanity. I finally decide to go to Ankara as Asef has done. It's probably pointless, but maybe the myth really happened. Maybe I'll be lucky and see Mersey.

At six I go to the police station. Officer Ibtehal is there, having his coffee. As I leave the room after signing the book he says suspiciously, 'You've come early today.'

'I couldn't sleep, Officer.' I try to avoid eye contact with him.

I go home, change my clothes and put on sunglasses and a hat I found in a garbage bin. I check myself in the mirror: I look like a KGB spy who's been sacked for poor performance. I go to the bus terminal at seven-thirty to get the eight-o'clock bus, glancing around to make sure nobody notices me. I plan to wait until all the passengers are on the bus and then when it's about to leave,

I'll approach the driver and ask for a seat. Usually in this situation you're seated at the back without a ticket, which means your name isn't recorded anywhere. I remember hearing my father talk about people doing this on his bus.

I look at my watch: it's seven-fifty. I see the bus is almost ready to go so I start walking slowly towards it. I look around again and see Officer Ibtehal with a young police officer arriving at the terminal. My heart racing, I keep walking while surreptitiously watching Ibtehal as he heads directly for the bus to Ankara. I stroll past it and continue on towards the exit. I'm almost there when I look back: Ibtehal has got on the bus and is checking the passengers. I speed up and arrive home in less than thirty minutes. I go inside, shut the door and drop to the floor.

Two weeks after my first attempt, I try again to go to Ankara. This time I'm much more cautious. During those two weeks I've been going to the police station at six-thirty every morning, so Officer Ibtehal gets the impression I've become an early-morning person. I wear my KGB uniform again and when I get to the bus terminal I duck into the bathroom to shave off my beard and moustache – a blasphemy, of sorts. I've always had a well-trimmed beard and getting rid of it feels as if I'm taking my clothes off in public.

The bus for Ankara is almost full when I see a man who looks like Ibtehal. He's not in police uniform, but I'm still suspicious. I sneak closer to him, and I realise he's the fisherman who sold us the river fish in the bazaar – if you can describe those tiny creatures as 'fish'.

The bus starts moving and the attendant sticks his head out and yells, 'Ankara! Ankara!'

I look around again. I can't see any signs of any policemen so I run over. 'Ankara?'

'Yallah!' yells the attendant, his voice much bigger than his stature.

I climb up and walk to the back but there are no seats. As the bus moves out of the terminal I try to avoid eye contact with everyone but I know I look awkward standing in the aisle. After a few minutes the attendant finally comes over and tells me to sit on another passenger's luggage. When we leave the outskirts of Çankiri, I exhale in relief.

The bus travels smoothly. There are about forty passengers, and a few kids cry every now and then. Suddenly I notice Barish two rows in front of me, but he can't see me unless he turns around. Though he's a nice man, I can't afford him knowing I went to Ankara without permission. News spreads fast in Çankiri. I keep my sunglasses on, even though I'm sure if Barish did see me he wouldn't recognise me. I don't think even Newsha would recognise me without my beard.

I close my eyes and try to relax. I remember a time when I was with my father in his bus, and we were driving through a mountain range. It was a spring morning and a refreshing rain had fallen the night before.

'Look,' my father said, pointing at a sea of red on the plain below the mountains.

'What's that?' I asked.

'Siavash's blood,' he murmured. 'Siavash was one of Iran's greatest heroes. He sacrificed his life for love, and for our country. Every year after the first spring rain millions of red poppies blossom in honour of Siavash.'

I stared at the plain, completely mesmerised and lost in admiration of Siavash. I felt proud of my homeland and of my father, who knew so much about our history. I thought, When I grow up, I will tell all these stories to my own son.

Later on that trip, my father took a small grapevine from the side of the road. When we got home he planted it in our tiny yard and for many years it gave us juicy red grapes. Ah, my father, I think, please forgive me for not having a chance to say goodbye to you before I left Iran.

My reverie is interrupted when, about thirty minutes from Ankara, the bus suddenly pulls over.

'Checkpoint!' the attendant yells out.

I stop breathing. I know there are occasional checkpoints on the road but I didn't expect there'd be one today.

'Cumhuriyet Bayrami!' says the man in front of me to his friend. I then realise that this is the day Turkey commemorates Ataturk's declaration of a republic. I sit on the bus hating myself, my life and my destiny.

I notice several special armed forces personnel at the checkpoint inspecting other vehicles. Two soldiers get on the bus – one stands in the aisle while the other walks down it, looking at the passengers. He points at one young man then another, both of whom have long beards and are wearing traditional Muslim clothing, and demands they show him their identification. He comes to the end of the bus and I can feel my stomach churning. I try to stay calm but it's impossible.

The soldier says to the man in front of me, 'Take your sunglasses off and show me your ID.'

He checks the man's papers and gives them back to him. The soldier looks at me. I take off my sunglasses and hat and return his gaze, knowing that if I avoid eye contact he'll get suspicious. I feel the same way I did twenty years ago when I hid Ali Mazaheri in my father's bus.

But suddenly he turns around, walks to the front of the bus and both soldiers get off. I wonder if it was shaving my beard that saved me. Perhaps they were looking for Islamic hardliners, in case of a terrorist attack on the anniversary of Turkey becoming a secular republic. I can only guess. The bus starts moving again but my limbs are completely paralysed. I begin to love my destiny once more.

Finally we reach Ankara. As I climb down the bus steps the attendant wishes me luck with a cheeky expression. He expects a tip, as if I'm a business-class passenger getting off an Airbus. I need to be careful; there are a lot of police and soldiers in the streets, and I look around to make sure no one's watching me. I get on a minibus and in less than half an hour I'm in front of the UN building. It's as crowded as ever and I walk up and down conversing here and there with some Iranians. I fall into conversation with Jabbar, who's come to Turkey from Lebanon. I tell him I'm an Iranian Muslim and he says he is too, obviously proud of his faith.

He points at the UN and says, 'I hate them. They all work for the Americans and the Jews. I had my interview ten months ago and still no results.'

'Can I ask what happened to you in Lebanon?'

'I'd been in Afghanistan fighting for the mujahedin, for Islam, until things went bad: the Taliban got out of hand, lots of us were killed. So I escaped to Lebanon.' He tells me he wants to go to America, Canada or Australia.

Jabbar is not the first Muslim I've met with a contradictory attitude towards the West. Quite a few consider Western society, especially America, the enemy of Islam and human civilisation, but at the same time they're desperate to migrate to a Western country – preferably America. Their main excuses are safety and a better job. After being rejected by the UN most of them go back to their original countries, without being persecuted – because they were never in real danger in the first place. I've even met people who, while waiting for their results at the UN, go back to their homeland and then return with food and other necessities from home.

I say goodbye to Jabbar and wish him luck.

It's an extremely cold afternoon and the weather gets worse by the minute. My toes are numb in my shoes and I keep my hands in my pockets. By five o'clock almost everyone has disappeared and it's getting dark. A police car turns into the street. I start walking, pretending I'm just a passer-by. As it drives past I see that the officers are checking the UN building. The car continues down the street. I begin to shiver.

By five-thirty no one has come out of the building but there are still some lights on inside. Minutes later the main gate opens and two labourers drag out a large object and drop it onto the footpath. When they go back inside I walk closer to it, using my cigarette lighter to see it more clearly. It's a carpet folded into a square. I lift up a corner of it – it's the worn-out yellow one from the waiting room. Maybe they're doing some renovations. I go back to the other side of the street and wait another few minutes. Most of the lights are off now and I grasp just how pointless the whole trip has been. Of course the officers aren't going to risk their safety by using the front gate; I even said this to Asef. I feel stupid. I touch my cold, shaved face. I wish I could cry or scream. Now I understand why that Kurdish man stitched his lips together. I desperately hope I never get to that point.

I go back to the carpet. I decide to take it with me and put it in our living room, to stop our feet sticking to the frozen concrete floor during winter. Yes, at least I can do this one thing. The kids will love it. I'm thinking about how to get it to Çankiri when a utility truck pulls up next to me. Two Turkish men get out, look at the carpet and say something to each other. I realise they're collecting used goods from the street to sell them in places like Ulus. I put my foot on the carpet and say to one of them, 'Bu benim.' It means, 'This is mine.'

He jumps towards me and pushes me so hard I fall to the ground. I repeat 'Bu benim, bu benim' and the other man punches me under my right eye. I see a flash of light and almost pass out but I crawl quickly over to the carpet and grip the corners as hard as I can. The other man starts trying to pull me off it while the first man punches me in the ribs and stomach. The pain in my abdomen is excruciating but I'm not going to let these Turks take my carpet from me. 'Bu benim!'

Eventually the men back off. They kick me in the guts one last time, swearing, and get back in their car and drive off. I stay on the carpet for a few minutes. My head is throbbing and my stomach aches badly. Each breath comes with a sharp pain in my chest. Finally I stand up, feeling dizzy, and look around. I have to get out of this street as soon as I can, before a police car comes. I try to pick the carpet up but it's extremely heavy. I drag it behind me to the main street. I can't get on a minibus with this enormous object so I hail a taxi. The driver says he can take me and the carpet to the bus terminal for twenty dollars. This is so expensive I consider abandoning the carpet, but the wellbeing of my daughers is too important, so I agree.

Before I get in he asks me where I'm from. 'Iran,' I murmur.

I wait for him to just take off but he says, 'My son-in-law is from Iran.' He gets out of the taxi and grabs a corner of the carpet. 'Yallah!' Together we lift it and put it in the boot. When we arrive at the bus terminal he accepts ten dollars from me and says, 'All the best.' It's still a lot of money, but I'm so grateful for the driver's generosity.

I shuffle into the terminal, dragging the carpet behind me, and can feel the other passengers staring at me. I look like I'm homeless. I'm covered in sweat and bruises and am gasping for air. I still have to go another hundred metres before I'll reach the last bus for Çankiri. I feel like I'm about to collapse when suddenly the carpet feels much lighter. I look back and there's a Turkish man with a long beard and traditional clothes pushing it for me.

'Thank you so much, sir,' I say to him.

'That's fine, brother,' he replies. I notice his two sons and his wife, whose face is covered with a burqa, walking behind him. I make sure my Star of David is hidden in my shirt. When we finally reach the bus I say to the kind man, 'Zahmet,' which means, 'Trouble.'

He turns to me with a smile and says, 'Rahmet,' which means, 'Blessing.'

The kindness of this stranger on such a horrible night, with my heart overtaken by sorrow and darkness, suddenly gives me a ray of hope. I put the carpet in the luggage compartment of the bus and climb aboard. When we get to Çankiri I drag the carpet as quickly as I can to a backstreet near the police station and hide it, before going in to sign the register. Thankfully, Ibtehal's shift is over and another officer is behind the desk. Though I notice him glancing at the bruise on my face, he doesn't ask me how I got it. I leave the station, retrieve the carpet, and begin the long walk home. When I eventually haul it inside the unit, I pass out from exhaustion.

TWELVE

I have five hundred dollars left in the bank. Thank God we're not paying rent, but food and other expenses are costing us about one hundred and fifty dollars a month. Occasionally we can afford vegetables and rice. I know that our money will run out in a few months and I am starting to panic. I have to generate some kind of income while we wait to hear from the UN. We're in a sinking ship.

It's a Thursday night in late autumn, seven weeks after my interview, and Asef and his family are visiting us. He's as worried as I am about money.

'I know this builder – he's constructing a three-storey building in Yildiz Sokak and needs labourers,' Asef says.

'Do you think he'd give us a job?'

'I can ask him.'

Two days later Asef tells me that the builder, Yashar, wants us to work for him.

We turn up at the construction site very early the next morning. Another four workers are also there, all Turkish. Soon Yashar arrives and tells Asef and me that our job is to put the bricks in a wheelbarrow and take them up to the bricklayer on the second level via some temporary steps. We are to work from six in the morning until seven at night and the pay is twenty dollars a week. It's pathetic but better than nothing. We agree to start straight away.

On our second day, during our lunch, the Turkish labourers tell us they get paid twenty-five dollars a day. Asef and I look at each other. He mutters to me, 'We have no choice; nobody else will give us work. If the police find out a Turkish citizen has employed us they'll shut down their business for six months. So let's just be grateful and do our jobs.' He resents the situation as much as I do.

It's difficult for me to wake up at five to go to work because I don't get to sleep until midnight, or even later, after translating *The Calendars of Ancient Aryans* all night. Labouring is very hard and unsafe work; we perspire despite the cold air and our fingers and toes are constantly numb. We get a fifteen-minute lunch break to eat the dates and bread our wives have packed in cloths for us. The Turkish workers make jokes about Asef and me all the time.

Two weeks after we've started, one of these workers on the second level sends me back down because he's decided the bricks I've brought up are not the right ones. I know he's just being a prick but I can't do anything. Asef does try to confront him, though, and the whole thing turns into a violent scene. Eventually the foreman intervenes and gets the Turkish men to agree to let me keep working. The Turks are angry about Asef and me because they know we work for less than a quarter of their wages, and they're worried about losing their jobs.

Every evening when I get home I am beyond exhausted. My hands are covered with blisters and my feet ache. Azita tries to be supportive and help me overcome my humiliation.

'Kooshyar, I know how hard this is for you but it's only for a few months. Then we'll be free and have an amazing life,' she tells me while massaging my legs. 'Someone told me yesterday that her cousin was an asylum seeker who spent two years in Turkey, but when she was finally moved to Sweden she was given a unit with a fridge and furniture. And listen to this – when she arrived, there was a big jug of orange juice in the fridge. Imagine that!'

Every Saturday, when we finish for the week, Yashar checks everything and pays the Turkish workers, but when Asef and I ask for our wages he says, 'I'll pay you next week – I'm a bit short of cash at the moment.' After a month of this, Asef and I agree to demand our money.

'We have family here and we really need some cash. It's been four weeks,' I say to Yashar.

'Can you please pay us?' Asef says after me.

Yashar reaches into his pocket and takes out some notes. He counts five dollars and gives it to Asef and then the same amount to me.

'Is that it?' I ask.

'That's it. If you're not happy, don't turn up next week.' Yashar walks away.

'Yashar, please wait,' Asef yells, running after him, but Yashar gets into his car and leaves. We shuffle home, our pride deeply wounded.

It's fifty-seven days since my interview. I count each day, just like the Count of Monte Cristo imprisoned in the Chateau d'If. When I ask Officer Ibtehal whether there's a fax for me he usually doesn't respond, a fat cat ignoring an emaciated mouse.

Winter has come early, as tonight it's snowing heavily. I look through the window at the blizzard – the river has disappeared under a thick frozen blanket. A strong gust shakes the naked trees. Even our yellow carpet has frosted but I have to wait until midnight to dismantle the electricity meter so I can turn on the heater.

Azita calls out to me from the other room, where she's changing Niloofar. When I go in she says, 'Niloofar's burning.' I touch our daughter's forehead: it's as hot as a furnace. 'She hasn't eaten or passed urine for hours, and she's so sleepy.'

'Is she coughing? Or does she have diarrhoea?' I ask.

'No, she's just lethargic and feverish.'

I pull up Niloofar's shirt and check her tummy. There's no rash but she grimaces when I gently press her lower abdomen.

'I think she might have a urinary tract infection. It's common in little girls, but she's probably got it because we're not using proper nappies,' I say guiltily. I look at Niloofar – her eyes are closed. I know that urinary sepsis can kill a baby in two hours. 'She needs intravenous antibiotics,' I say, and start wrapping her in a blanket.

'Where are you going?' asks Azita.

'To the hospital.' I pick Niloofar up.

'But it's snowing. And it's ten o'clock at night and the hospital is more than forty-five minutes away. Besides, the dogs will kill you. We need someone to give us a lift.'

'Do you know someone who'd give an evsiz a lift at this time of night?' I ask her sarcastically.

I hold Niloofar against my chest and race out the door. As soon as I leave the building a strong, freezing wind hits me. I try to cover her face – I'm worried the blizzard will cause her to go into respiratory arrest. Even I'm finding it hard to breathe. I use all my strength to run but I'm going against the wind and the snow is as high as my knees. Adonai, I pray, please save my daughter.

I cross the bridge. Stray dogs begin to bark behind me. Dogs in this part of the world are not pets; they're worse than wolves. I try to speed up but my legs sink into the snow. I gather every quantum of energy I have left and push forward, hunched over to protect Niloofar from the gale. I flick the blanket back momentarily: she hasn't opened her eyes. I put my ear to her mouth. She's breathing so I cover her face again and keep going.

I reach a deserted, dangerous part of Çankiri. It's still another few kilometres to the hospital. There are some brown spots ahead, getting closer and bigger. More wild dogs, desolate and ravenous. I keep going and the dogs come to a halt. I'm now so close I can smell the stench of their frosted hides. I remember my father's advice: 'If a wolf is about to attack you, don't run away or it will chase you and sink its teeth into your neck. Just stop, crouch down and stare into its eyes.'

I'm terrified, but I cease running. There are five of them and they're enormous. One has nasty ulcers around his mouth. They stand there growling, motionless but fierce. I hug Niloofar tighter. I'm not going to let these ferocious animals get my daughter, even if they tear me apart. They begin to form a circle around me. I summon my hope and courage and stare into their eyes. Suddenly one of them starts to come closer. I slowly bend down and make a barking sound, as loud as I can. The creature stops, its eyes still piercing me, and then goes back. I bark again and carefully step towards them. They all move backwards slightly. I'm now right in the middle of the pack; I can see the wet on their noses, their salivating mouths. I keep my pace – not too fast, not too slow – and advance past them. When I'm a few metres away I straighten my back and speed up. Then, when I'm certain they're not following me, I run.

After another twenty minutes I finally see the sign for the hospital. I rush into Emergency at close to eleven o'clock. A nurse asks for my details, and as soon as she finds out I'm an Iranian asylum seeker her behaviour changes. I take out some cash from my pocket and say, 'I promise I will pay. Just get the doctor, please.'

'Wait here,' she demands and disappears. There are three other patients in the waiting room, including an old woman coughing badly and a middle-aged man vomiting into a bucket. The nurse comes back with a young security guard. Chatting and giggling, they go out again for a cigarette. I wait another ten minutes in profound anxiety, knowing Niloofar's chances of survival are dropping every second.

'Nurse! Anybody! Please help!' I yell out in frustration.

The security guard appears. 'Be quiet or I'll kick you out.'

'My daughter is very sick. She's going to die —'

'I said quiet!' He glares at me and walks away, disappearing behind a pale green door. When the nurse comes back ten minutes later, her lipstick is smudged all around her mouth, making her look like a naughty little girl who's been scoffing a pink cake. She attends to the vomiting man and I rush over to her.

'Please, Nurse, for God's sake, help my daughter.'

The nauseated man says, 'I'll be fine, check this man's daughter.'

Finally the nurse looks at Niloofar.

'She has a high temperature,' I say.

The nurse puts her hand on Niloofar's face and whispers 'ateş' – 'fire'. Then she asks me her name. I tell her and she says it loudly while shaking her, but Niloofar doesn't respond.

'Okay, come with me,' the nurse says, heading through the pale green door.

I quickly thank the man before following her. I walk past the security guard, who's hastily adjusting his fly.

There are five beds in the ward, three occupied by patients. Seeing needles and monitors and smelling chlorhexidine and Betadine remind me of my years working in Iran. The doctor on duty, a young registrar, walks in. The nurse takes Niloofar from me and puts her on a bed. I watch the doctor examine her and realise how inexperienced he is. He also seems very tired but I try not to interfere.

'Check her temperature,' he tells the nurse.

'It's 41.2,' she says to the doctor, a worried look on her face.

He takes out his stethoscope and checks her chest. Then he looks into her ears and mouth. He doesn't bother to ask me anything about her symptoms or her medical history.

'Excuse me, Doctor, I can tell you something about her illness,' I say politely. The doctor ignores me and tells the nurse to give Niloofar a paracetamol suppository. I know that might lower her temperature but it's not going to fix the infection. I stand there watching the nurse applying the suppository. The doctor disappears into another room. Another ten minutes pass.

'Excuse me, is the doctor coming back?' I ask the nurse, who's now preparing some intravenous fluids for another patient.

'I'm not sure,' she says without looking at me.

I'm about to lose my patience but I say to her gently, 'I think my daughter needs antibiotics.'

'I'm busy. And stay there quietly or I'll call security,' she says.

I go back to Niloofar. Her breathing has slowed down and become shallower. I'm not going to let her die in this idiotic Çankiri slaughterhouse. I rush over to the room the doctor entered and see him lying on a bed.

'My daughter has a urinary tract infection. She's only six months old. I'm a doctor too so I know what I'm talking about. Please —'

'Get out! Get out now!' He leaps up and pushes me out the door then slams it shut behind me.

I stand in the Emergency ward, hopeless and restless. I frantically look around. The nurse has gone to the other side of the department, maybe to make sure the security guy is okay. I spot a medication trolley, and hurry over to see if there's a small paediatric cannula. I find one and go back to Niloofar, pull up her sleeve and successfully insert it. Now I need some fluids and a vial of ceftriaxone, the wide-spectrum antibiotic. In the cart I find ten millilitres of normal saline, which I slowly inject into Niloofar. This should save her from haemodynamic shock.

The nurse comes towards me and I pretend to be waiting for the doctor, while trying to hide the medical equipment I've taken. But she doesn't even glance in my direction. As soon as she's disappeared again I race back to the drug trolley but there are no antibiotics there. I scan the ward and go over to the main cupboard, but it's locked and I can't see the key anywhere. I think, The nurse will have a key. Though I'll be deported for it, I'm going to get it from her, even if I have to use force.

'What are you doing here?' I spin around, startled. A grey-haired man wearing a tie and a stethoscope is approaching. He must be a senior doctor.

'Doctor, please help me, for God's sake!'

'What's going on?' he asks.

'I'm a doctor from Iran. My daughter is sick – she's six months old with urinary sepsis and she's going to die. Please believe me, she needs intravenous antibiotics urgently.'

'Where is she?' he asks.

I take him over to Niloofar and pull the blanket off so he can examine her. He seems to be competent and knowledgeable and I begin to feel hopeful. 'How long has she been sick?' he asks.

'We noticed it two hours ago.'

'Has she had a urinary tract infection before? Or any other conditions?'

'No.'

'Did you put the cannula in?' he asks.

'Yes.' I'm afraid he'll be furious.

'Good job. I'm sure that lousy registrar wouldn't be able to cannulate an infant with collapsed veins,' he says.

In a matter of minutes, antibiotics are going through Niloofar's body. Before the senior doctor leaves, he says to me, 'I'm Dr Mehmet and I'm the head of Emergency here. If you need anything just ask the nurse to contact me. I've told her to give your daughter special care.'

I thank him, my heart bursting with gratitude. I stay beside Niloofar's bed all night. It takes eighteen hours for her to respond, but she improves and even produces some urine. When I'm eventually able to take her home, I'm told I don't need to pay anything.

I walk back to our unit with Niloofar in my arms. She's breathing normally and no longer has a high temperature. I'm so grateful to the doctor, and to my Adonai. I hope that one day I'll practise medicine again, wherever we end up, and save the lives of those who have no hope.

It's now sixty-nine days since my interview – another bitter, glacial morning. Azita and I try to mop up all the water that's come through the window during the night. At eight-thirty there's a knock on the door.

Could this be the police again? I've heard that they're checking units to make sure the electricity meters haven't been rigged. I've already been out to turn on the meter's counter but if they notice the broken seal I'll be arrested.

There's another knock. 'It's me. Asef.'

I open the door. He's standing in the doorway with a look of shock on his face.

'Is everything okay?' It's unusual for him to be here so early.

'I was signing at the police station and Ibtehal told me . . .'

My heart skips a beat. 'What?'

'He said you have a fax.'

I can't breathe, and feel as if all the blood has gone from my veins. I sit down.

Azita gasps behind me. 'Is it from the UN?'

'It must be. They're the only ones who fax the station,' Asef says.

It takes me a while to gather my courage. Azita says, 'Good news or bad news, you have to see it, Kooshyar. I'll stay here with the children. You go by yourself.'

When I finally step out the door Azita says, 'Pray! Pray to Adonai!' This surprises me and I smile at her, grateful. I pray all the way there, not seeing anything or anyone. I'm more fearful than a man going to the firing squad. If the fax says my case has been rejected, this could be the last night I see Azita, Newsha and Niloofar for some time.

I walk into the police station. Officer Ibtehal has his legs resting on the desk, as usual. 'Merhaba, Officer Ibtehal,' I say. Today his face is behind a book, not a newspaper, and I glance at the cover. It says something that would translate as *Mouth Service: An Erotic Story*. The perfect book for Ibtehal. He ignores me. I want to ask him about the fax straight away but I know he'll just ignore me. I look at the register and reach into my pocket for my pen but I've forgotten it – on this of all mornings. He'll get angry with me if I ask for one; he might even refuse to show me the fax. He turns another page of his book and a minute passes. I'm getting more and more anxious.

When Officer Ibtehal senses me looking at him he puts his beloved book down and stares at me with cold eyes. He has a pen behind his right ear. 'You need a pen, do you?' he asks me impatiently. 'Get out of my office and come back with one.' He resumes reading.

Distracted by nerves, I walk aimlessly in the streets until I find myself in front of a grocery shop. I go in and buy their cheapest pen then return to the police station. Officer Ibtehal is still there, reading his book. I sign my name then stand there in silence. I don't want to annoy him by asking about the fax so I wait for almost five minutes. He flips the page and keeps reading so I walk to the door and am about to leave. Is this all some sort of joke?

'Kooshyar, there's a fax for you,' he yells from behind *Mouth Service*. 'Salim!' A skinny junior officer comes out of the other room and salutes him. 'Get that fax for this evsiz.' Salim goes back out and returns with a folded piece of paper. When I take it from him my hands are shaking.

I thank him and leave the station. I can't bring myself to read it in front of Ibtehal or in the street, so I grip it firmly and walk home, constantly whispering, 'Adonai.'

When Azita opens the door I give her the fax. 'You read it,' I say.

'But it's in English,' she says.

'I'm sorry, I forgot.' I take it back from her and we go to the other room. I don't want the children to know anything about this.

I clear my throat, take a deep breath and try to stop trembling. 'It says, "Dear Mr Kooshyar Karimi, following your interview on 12 September 1999, the UNHCR has checked the information you provided and has reached the conclusion that you were subjected to human rights abuses by the Iranian regime. Therefore, the UNHCR has decided to recognise you as a political refugee. From 27 November 1999 you will be under our protection, and arrangements will be made to transfer you safely to a third country. After receiving this letter you have seven days to present at the UNHCR office in Ankara to have a brief interview about your financial situation and the transfer process."'

Azita screams and jumps up and down while I dance around like a lunatic. Newsha runs in. 'What's going on?' I pick her up and spin her in the air. 'Guess what, Newsha? Guess what?'

'What, Baba jan?' she says excitedly. She can see the joy in my eyes, the joy that disappeared when I was first kidnapped by MOIS almost three years ago.

'We're going! We're going to Disneyland!'

Newsha's face lights up with the biggest smile I've ever seen in my life. 'When, Baba jan, when?'

'Soon! Very soon, I promise!'

That night I'm still in a pleasant state of shock and disbelief. At eight o'clock I go out for a walk. It's extremely cold but to me the world feels nice and warm. As I stroll I whisper, 'Thank you, Adonai. I'll always keep my faith in you.' Then I can't contain myself and start yelling, 'I love you, my Adonai! I love life! I love the UN!'

When I return home Azita says we have to let Asef and Soosan know about our success. Though I know she's right, I feel very uncomfortable. How can we express our happiness to them when they're still stuck here waiting? Wouldn't it be mean?

'I know you're worried about upsetting Asef but I'm sure he'll be happy for us,' says Azita.

And so we get the kids dressed and head out into the snow. The good thing about asylum seekers is that you don't need to let them know you're going to visit them. They're so lonely and desperate that anyone knocking on their door is welcome – unless it's the police, of course.

When Asef opens the door I can't hide my joy. He immediately knows everything and gives me a big smile.

'Congratulations, brother!' And we hug each other. Azita and Soosan hold each other too and we all cry hard. Newsha wants to tell Navid and Neema we're going to Disneyland but they're asleep.

'Kooshyar jan, this is the happiest night we've had since arriving in Çankiri. Believe me, we're as thrilled as if it were our own result.' I so admire his magnanimity. Asef and I plan to celebrate by getting drunk tomorrow evening but we don't have much hope of accomplishing this. I only have about three hundred and fifty dollars left and Asef has even less, so we can't justify spending more than twenty dollars on alcohol.

We go to the liquor shop the following day anyway. After searching through the vast array of drinks on display we realise that twenty dollars will only buy six cans of beer, an alcohol content of less than half a bottle of wine. Next to us a Turkish man is picking up fancy-looking bottles. How I envy him and wish he was my friend. I put the cans of beer on the counter next to his big bag of rum, Scotch and Smirnoff vodka. While the man's still selecting, the teenage cashier takes the twenty dollars from me and hands me the big bag of bottles by mistake. In a moment of impulse, I walk out of the shop, fast. Asef is talking to me about his fascination with the liquor shop but I focus on moving as quickly as I can without seeming suspicious.

'Slow down! What's the rush?' he asks.

'Just keep up,' I whisper, and go faster. I know I've taken a huge risk, but it's too late to go back. Besides, my desire to celebrate tonight is overwhelming. As soon as we reach a corner I start to run. Asef, who is almost ten years older than I am, finds it hard to match my pace. 'What's going on?' he asks, panting.

'Just keep running and don't look back!' I sprint as if an army of police were after us.

In less than half an hour we arrive home, with Asef gasping for air. I sit on the floor, open the big plastic bag and take out the bottles. I start laughing like a lunatic. A few hours later Asef is so drunk he's making sheep sounds and crawling on the floor, while I'm dancing and yelling, 'Fuck Officer Ibtehal!' Azita's shrieking with laughter and Soosan's vomiting out the window.

Next morning we're all hung-over. I've no idea when or how we got to sleep, but we're still euphoric.

'The best night of my life,' Asef says as we head to the police station to sign.

'Me too.' I put my arm around his shoulder. 'Asef jan, I know your fax is coming. I have no doubt.'

We arrive at the station and sign the book, this time using Asef's pen. In the last two days I've been so focused on celebrating that I haven't yet asked for permission to go to Ankara. I show my fax to Officer Ibtehal. 'I need to go to Ankara for this interview, please,' I say to him, though I know he's well aware of the process.

He drops the fax onto the desk. 'I can't give you permission.' And he keeps reading his book.

I'm speechless. If I don't go to this interview in six days my case might be cancelled.

'Did you hear me?' he says aggressively.

I'm about to protest but Asef pulls my sleeve and whispers, 'Don't.'

As we leave the station Asef says, 'He's not working tomorrow. Come back and ask the other officer – he'll let you go.'

'How do you know?'

'I've been here much longer than you. Every second Thursday is Ibtehal's day off.' And we both smile.

Azita and I sit up late into the night talking about our future. 'I can't believe we're finally going to America,' I say excitedly, but she shakes her head.

'No, Kooshyar, not America,' she says adamantly. 'I know you want to go because it's modern and has a lot of Jews, but I'm not willing to move there.'

'Why not?' I'm stunned.

'It's dangerous. Everyone has a gun and there's too much crime. I've been through enough and I need to ask you this one last favour. Please don't take us to America.'

The last thing I expect, especially now we're going to be free, is her ignorant, implacable stubbornness. On the other hand, Azita has been with me every step of the way so far, caring for our children, and though she's complained at times she's never made good on her threat to go back to Iran with them. I owe her something. 'Okay. Where would you like to go, then?' I ask her. 'But don't forget that the UN will ultimately send us wherever they want to.'

'I know that but when they ask where you'd prefer, I want you to say Australia.' I have heard it's a beautiful, safe place so I agree.

The next day I climb on board the bus for Ankara, legally, after getting written permission from the police that morning. In a few hours I'm at the UN, showing the guards my fax. They escort me inside and I'm treated with respect, which is a strange but wonderful feeling.

Even so, I have to wait an hour before being interviewed. This time it's with a young English officer.

'Mr Karimi, congratulations. You've been recognised as a political refugee and the UN is going to send you to a third country.'

'Thank you so much.'

'Unfortunately this will take some time and you'll need to be patient. We can apply for Norway, Finland, Sweden, Canada, America or Australia but we have no idea which of these countries is going to give you permanent residency. You can tell us your preference and the UN will approach that country first, but there's no guarantee they'll accept you. So, do you have a preference?'

'Yes, sir, I would like to be sent to Australia.'

'And why is that?' he says, ready to type my response.

I explain that I know Australia is a democratic, multicultural country, one that respects people regardless of their ethnicity or religion. It will also be safe for my children. The officer nods but says, 'The process is longer for Australia – around twelve months – twice as long as for Norway or America.' He raises his eyebrows, waiting to see if I've changed my mind. But I remember my promise to Azita, and I imagine Newsha and Niloofar walking to school in that beautiful land and enjoying freedom and respect.

'That's okay. I would love to go to Australia, even if it takes another twelve months or more,' I tell him.

Then he asks about my current living expenses, and after doing some calculations he tells me the UN can pay me a hundred and twenty dollars a month. 'I know this isn't much but it's all we can offer.' Even though it won't cover all our costs, getting this money will be such a relief.

By the time I get back to Çankiri it's nine o'clock. I give Azita the good news about the financial assistance and the bad news about the extra twelve months of waiting.

'Wherever they send us, though, we'll go and start a new life and Newsha and Niloofar will be happy,' I say and Azita agrees.

Time slows down over the next few weeks. Knowing I'm going to leave Turkey makes every day drag on and on. I continue to feel unsafe here and am constantly aware that if I do anything wrong I'll be deported. I have to be cautious; I have to survive here for another six to twelve months.

Two months pass with no news. My own money has nearly run out, and inflation is so high that even with the allowance from the UN, we can still only afford to eat bread, eggs and potatoes, and sometimes rice. Not having enough meat and fruit for so long has made Newsha emaciated and anaemic. Although Niloofar is now eating solid food, I can't afford to give her a decent meal and I'm worried this will permanently damage her health.

'We have to feed them some meat and some fruit,' Azita tells me one night.

I go to the only supermarket in Çankiri and find the meat section. After glancing at the security camera, I pick up two packets of mince: one is a hundred grams for a dollar, the other is one kilogram for eight dollars. I take them over to a part of the shop the camera can't see and peel off the price stickers, replacing one with the other one, and then put the hundred-gram packet back on the shelf. I walk to the checkout and the woman scans the one-kilogram packet of mince. 'One dollar.'

I pay for it and walk out. My heart is about to jump out of my mouth. This is the first meat we've eaten in four months.

After Azita's fallen asleep that night I take a pillowcase and tiptoe to the grocery shop downstairs. As quietly as possible I pull the covers off the fruit boxes. I'm mesmerised by the shiny apples and large mandarins, and put five of each in my pillowcase. Then I notice a set of six plastic knives and spoons, and I take that too. When I go back to our unit and place everything on the floor I can't help but feel exhilarated.

Over the next three months I steal mince from the supermarket once a week and fruit from Barish's shop once a fortnight. I have no choice – my daughters' welfare is at stake – but I feel terrible about stealing from Barish, so each time I only take four mandarins and four apples, just enough to keep the girls relatively healthy. I promise myself that one day I'll send him some money and my apologies. Then one day while I'm at Barish's shop buying bread as usual, he tells another customer that someone's been stealing fruit from his shop.

'But how is that possible?' asks the customer.

'I don't know – I sleep right next to my shop every night. The bastard must be a professional,' says Barish.

I feel a shiver down my spine. I had no idea Barish's unit is behind his shop. Every time I've filled my pillowcase he's been only a few steps away. I go back upstairs and tell Azita there'll be no fruit for a while.

The next month, while I'm signing at the police station, Officer Ibtehal murmurs, 'There's a thief in this town. I wonder who that could be.' He puts his book down and gives me a suspicious look.

'A thief?' I repeat, trying to sound innocent.

'Things have been going missing from some shops.' He stares at me. 'It must be one of the asylum seekers. Turks don't steal – they have pride.'

I wonder what pride has to do with poverty and malnutrition. 'I'm sure you'll catch him, Officer,' I say to this Turkish Sherlock Holmes and walk out.

As soon as I get home I grab the plastic spoons and knives I took from the grocery shop and hide them in my shirt. When it's dark, I go out and throw them into the river. I feel like a murderer destroying his victim's body parts.

A week later, at eleven at night, there's a violent banging on our door.

'Police!' I open the door and four policemen follow Officer Ibtehal inside. They search everywhere for anything illegal or suspicious. All they find is the heater. When Ibtehal asks what it is, I have to restrain myself from telling him it's a rocket launcher.

'Where did you get it from?' he asks.

'I made it.'

'Really? You made a brick and some wires, did you?' Officer Ibtehal is not the brightest man in Turkey.

'No, Officer, I found the brick and I bought the electric element. I attached them together with a piece of cable and we use it for cooking every now and then.'

'How did you know to do that?'

'I worked in the electronics industry back in Iran.'

He puts the heater back onto the floor and continues to inspect the rest of the house, waking up Newsha and Niloofar. Newsha panics and starts crying loudly. Azita tries to calm her down but I can see that her own face is full of anxiety.

'Check the meter,' says Ibtehal to one of the junior officers. My heart skips a beat. The officer goes out and looks up at the top of the doorway. The counter is spinning.

'It's working, Sergeant.'

Before they leave, Ibtehal stands in front of me and scowls. 'All asylum seekers are thieves; it's just a matter of time until they get caught.'

I say nothing. When I finally shut the door, I sit down on the floor and breathe again.

*

The weather is slowly improving so I don't need to interfere with the electricity meter as often, but I'm still stealing meat regularly from the supermarket. Every night before I do this I can't sleep, and each time I go through the checkout I hear Ibtehal's words in my head and become convinced that this is the moment when I'll be caught and sent back to Iran.

A few months after my last UNHCR interview I receive an envelope from them. I look at it all day with a mixture of anxiety and excitement but decide not to open it until the children are asleep. When I do, it's the best news: Australia has accepted our visa application. Azita and I celebrate in our small room quietly with a bottle of water.

The letter is five pages long and provides information about the country. The more I read, the more fascinated and excited I am. We sit there till two o'clock going through it together, with me translating for Azita. 'They have elections every three years. Can you believe it? And Sydney and Melbourne are always voted as two of the world's most liveable cities. What a gorgeous country.'

It also says I need to go to the Australian embassy in nine days for a brief interview. In the morning, when I'm at the police station, I show the letter to Ibtehal.

'So what?' He shrugs his fat shoulders.

'I need permission to go to the Australian embassy in Ankara, please,' I say courteously.

'Come back in eight days and apply then.' He hurls the letter onto his desk.

'But, sir —'

'Are you deaf? I said come back when you have your appointment!' he yells.

There's no point arguing with him. I leave depressed, knowing that Ibtehal's working every day until the interview. But as I walk home I resolve to find my way there, no matter what it takes.

The next day I go to the office of a telephone company that provides affordable calls overseas. When I enter, an old Turkish man is at the counter paying his bill. A large number of Turks work overseas, especially in Europe, and they send money back home to their families, so many people use companies like this instead of a home or mobile phone. After the old man's finished, I ask the young girl at the desk what the price is to call Iran.

'Minimum ten dollars for five minutes,' she says.

'But I only have three dollars.'

'I'm sorry.' She shakes her head.

'Please, it's very important. I have to call my mother. Can I just buy two minutes?'

'Let me ask my supervisor.' She takes off her telephone headset and goes to the other room. Shortly afterwards a Turkish man comes out.

'Minimum is ten dollars,' he says adamantly.

'Please, sir, I'm an asylum seeker. I need to make a call to Iran to say —'

'I'm sorry, I can't help you.' He returns to the other room.

I storm out, frustrated. I just want to make sure my mother is all right and tell her we're moving to Australia. I haven't had enough money to contact her, since she was arrested by MOIS.

I walk home, passing the small park. There are some Turkish kids playing and I notice Asef and his family sitting in a corner in the sun. Navid is waiting for a swing to be free so he can use it. He looks annoyed. I wave to Asef and he invites me to join them. After we say hello I tell him about the phone call.

'Here, come with me.' He stands up.

'Where are we going?'

'Just follow me.' He walks fast and in ten minutes we're at the mosque, which is packed with people praying. 'There's a man here who's helped me before,' Asef says, looking around. 'There he is.' And he rushes over to a Kurdish-looking man on the other side. 'Salam-al-alaykom, Jasim abi!'

'Alaykom-salam, Asef,' the man replies. Asef introduces us and tells him he needs a favour. Then he explains my situation. Jasim takes out his mobile phone and hands it to me. 'Here, brother. Use this.'

I'm shocked. The call will cost a fortune on the mobile. 'Thank you, Jasim abi, but I can't. It's very kind of you but —'

'Yallah, call your mother,' he insists.

I thank him again and take the phone before moving away to dial my mother's home number. I pray that what I said in my interview about the party means she's still alive.

After five rings I hear my mother's voice and feel profound relief.

'Hello, Maman jan. It's me, Kooshyar.'

'Kooshyar jan, are you okay? May Adonai be your protector! Where are you? Are you safe? I've been worried sick. Are Newsha and Niloofar okay?'

'Yes, Maman jan, yes, we're all okay. Are you?'

'Yes, I'm fine. I'm a tough woman, as you know.' Then she bursts into tears. 'They . . . they . . .'

I know she's trying to tell me MOIS tortured her, but I don't want her to say anything because her phone is tapped.

'Maman jan, are you all right?' I ask.

'Yes, but they've frozen all your accounts and taken everything you had – your furniture, your fridge, your TV, your books.'

'Don't worry, Maman jan. It doesn't matter as long as you're okay.'

'I'm fine, Kooshyar jan. Are you still in Turkey?'

'Yes, but in a little while we're going to a safer country.' I can't tell her where in case MOIS is listening. 'Maman jan, I'm sorry but I have to go. I just wanted to make sure you're okay. I'll call you soon from an amazing country.'

'Thanks be to Adonai,' she says, her voice full of joy. She whispers a Hebrew prayer down the line to keep me protected, and then exhales deeply.

I give the phone back to Jasim. 'I don't know how to thank you, brother.'

'Don't worry about it. Anytime,' he says with a smile and pats me on my shoulder. 'We're all brothers and sisters.'

On our way to the park Asef tells me that Jasim's father and brothers were executed by the Turkish government years ago.

'He's a very lonely man but he has the heart of an angel,' Asef says.

'How did you meet him?'

'When I was first sent to Çankiri I couldn't find a place to rent for five weeks, and we had to live in the park in the middle of summer. One night he came across us and offered to rent his unit to us. He's been my saviour.'

That night Asef and his family visit us. After the usual talk the women and children go to sleep and Asef and I sit up until late. For the first time he asks me guardedly about my story. Now that my case has been decided I feel confident sharing my story with Asef, so I tell him what happened to me in Iran.

Then Asef tells me his story. He was a successful engineer, the chief project manager for a big company in Tehran, but he was also a member of an underground communist group whose goal was to topple the regime and establish a socialist democratic government.

'One night we put flyers in houses around town, hundreds of them, but one of us was spotted by MOIS. He was arrested the next day, and then we all tried to escape. I was very lucky. The day after I left Iran the head of the group, a forty-year-old journalist with a wife and three kids, was imprisoned then made to appear in a show trial. Four days later he was executed.' I can see tears in Asef's eyes.

It's easy for me to imagine the profound sorrow of losing a member of your group, especially when you are in charge of their safety. The grief would stay with you forever.

THIRTEEN

I wake up at five o'clock on the day of my interview at the Australian embassy. I need to catch the first bus, at seven-thirty, to get there by midday; the only other bus to Ankara leaves at eleven. If I miss this appointment, I'll have to wait a few months for another one. I'm extremely nervous because I don't yet have permission to leave Çankiri. At six I arrive at the police station and a young officer is there.

'You'll have to wait for Officer Ibtehal,' he says indifferently.

'Do you know when he's coming?' I ask.

'Usually at seven.'

I wait in a corner. When it's finally seven, there's no sign of Ibtehal. I wait another five minutes then beg the young officer.

'Please, I have an appointment I've waited months for.'

'I can't help you.'

I wait another twenty minutes in absolute frustration; the bus is about to leave. Finally, fifteen minutes after it's gone, Ibtehal appears. He looks drained and unwell. The younger officer stands up and salutes him. Then Ibtehal stares at me, expecting a special greeting. So I say in English, 'You look as if five orangutans made you their sex toy last night.'

'What? Say it in Turkish!' he demands in fury.

'I hope you feel better soon.'

'What are you doing here anyway?' he asks.

'I need to catch the bus to Ankara. Please can you sign this permission letter?'

'Let me see it.'

I place the letter on the desk in front of him. He puts his cup of tea on it.

'So you need permission?' he says derisively. 'What for?'

'To go to the Australian embassy. The UNHCR has made an appointment for me, sir.'

'So you want to go to Australia?' He takes a sip of his tea then grins at the younger officer, who smirks back. 'Are you going to steal electricity in Australia too? And shoplift?'

'No, sir,' I whisper.

Officer Ibtehal looks at the letter, then at his watch. 'Your appointment is for twelve?'

'Yes, sir, and I've missed the bus.'

He signs the letter and throws it at me. 'There's always another bus.'

I grab the piece of paper and hurry out of the station, sweating with exasperation. I'll just have to catch the next bus and hope I can still be interviewed today.

I wait in the terminal until I get the bus at eleven. At two o'clock I'm in a taxi going to the Australian embassy. When we get there I ask the driver for a favour.

'Yes?' he says pleasantly.

'Could you please do the knot on my tie for me? I've never tried it before.' Ties are illegal in Iran because they're considered a symbol of Western culture. The taxi driver does up the tie I've borrowed from Asef. 'Nice,' he says, smiling. I pay him and run to the embassy, my long, wide, colourful tie waving like a sail.

It's two-thirty when I rush through the door. I'm so embarrassed at how late I am. I show my ID and am told to sit in the waiting room. A young man comes up to me and says in English, 'You're more than two hours late so your appointment has been cancelled. You'll have to come back another time.'

'But I can't – the police won't allow me. Please let me see someone today.'

'I have to ask you to leave.'

'But I've come all the way from Çankiri. I'm an asylum seeker – please let me see the officer.'

'I'm sorry but if you don't leave I'll call security.'

We're still arguing when a female voice interrupts us. 'Is this Dr Karimi?'

A woman in her mid-fifties is looking at us from the doorway of an office next to the waiting room. It takes a moment to realise she's addressed me by my title.

'Yes, this is Kooshyar Karimi, ma'am,' says the young man.

'Come in, Dr Karimi.' The man steps aside and I go into the office. There's a photo of an Australian landscape on the wall.

'I'm so sorry, ma'am. I had to get permission from the police and they kept me waiting for hours.'

'I know how horrible the Turkish police can be.' She smiles and I feel enormously relieved. I notice the right arm of her reading glasses is missing and feel even more respect for such a humble, unpretentious woman. 'I've studied your file from the UN, so you don't have to repeat all those details again. I already know how much you have gone through. Today will just be a quick interview.'

'Yes, ma'am.' She has a folder on her desk, which I guess is my file.

'May I ask why you have chosen Australia?'

'To be honest, because Australia is a democratic, free and safe country, and I want my children to grow up in such an environment.'

She nods. 'I've seen their photos; they're gorgeous. Now, I know you were a doctor in Iran. What would you like to do once you're living in Australia?'

'I'd like to practise medicine again, if possible.'

She raises her eyebrows. 'I must warn you that will be extremely hard. You'll have to pass a series of exams to get an Australian medical licence. It can take years.'

'I'm not scared of hard work, ma'am,' I reply firmly.

'Great,' she says, and smiles warmly. 'I'm assuming you will live in Australia permanently. Is that correct?'

'Yes, ma'am.'

'So if one day a country attacks Australia, what would you do?'

'I will go to war the same day.'

'Why?'

'Because Australia has given me a second chance to live, ma'am.' She smiles again.

'And will you miss your home?'

This question touches my heart deeply. 'Australia will be my home.'

Three more months pass without news. The woman who interviewed me said approval would take a lot of time and a lot of paperwork between the UNHCR, the Australian government and its embassy, and me. Every morning when Newsha wakes up she asks when we're going, and I try to keep her occupied and happy while we wait. I take her to the river to find rocks. It's a favourite pastime of ours; we especially like ones that are colourful, round and smooth. We keep them all in a glass jar we found in the street.

Sometimes I take her and Niloofar with me to sign at the police station and if I get a chance I put Niloofar on the swing on the way back. She loves it. Despite all the deprivation she's growing fast.

One day while we're at the park I notice a Persian-looking man holding a baby girl in his arms. When I walk over to introduce myself, I recognise him.

'Hello, Dariush. Long time no see.'

'How have you been, Kooshyar?'

Dariush is the asylum seeker I met outside the UN whose wife got cancer after giving birth to their daughter. He tells me, 'Marjan has had her second round of chemotherapy but she's not coping very well. She's so weak and has lost a lot of weight.' While Dariush is talking I look at the beautiful little girl in his arms and my heart aches. 'I've been trying to get permission to visit her in Ankara but this awful police officer always denies me. Last week when I saw Marjan she wanted to hold our daughter but the nurse wouldn't allow her because of the chemotherapy. It's so hard, Kooshyar, so hard.' Dariush breaks down.

'Stay strong, Dariush,' I say, gently gripping his arm. 'Your daughter needs you. I'm sure the UNHCR will help you – they're good people. You just need to be patient.'

Dariush simply nods and says, 'Thank you for listening to me,' before walking away.

I gather Newsha and Niloofar and we leave the park. The booth nearby is selling ice-creams again, instead of boiled beetroot during winter, but our savings has completely run out now and we're solely relying on the allowance from the UNHCR. I'm always looking in the streets for junk to turn into useful goods for our home. I've managed to make a clock, a crystal set, two chairs and an electric kettle. Yesterday I found a kitchen rangehood and took it home, removed the engine and made a panel out of some foam.

'What are you doing?' asked Azita.

'I'm making a fan. I'm going to change its panels so it will blow the air out.' We now have a small rotating motor that, when plugged into the power outlet, spins a foam panel that I have cut into the shape of a fan blade. It's attached to a fruit box I found in the street and is very ugly – just like our table – but it works perfectly.

'Wow, that's amazing!' says Asef when he visits us that night. This is our second summer in Turkey and his third. Asef hates the heat and can't afford a fan so he starts coming over every day to sit in front of mine.

Another month passes. I receive a letter from the Australian embassy telling us we all have to go to Ankara for medical tests.

Fortunately Ibtehal is on leave and the new officer gives me permission without any drama. When we're seen by Dr Noori in his surgery, he reads a brief report about my case then smiles and says, 'Ah, you're a doctor too, that will make things much easier and quicker.' His respectful manner makes me feel at ease. 'After I've examined you all, we'll then have to do chest X-rays as well as urine and blood tests. The Australian government wants to make sure you don't have any serious illnesses like HIV or tuberculosis.'

Dr Noori checks us thoroughly and, miraculously, we're all reasonably healthy. After he's finished he offers to give us a lift to the imaging and pathology building because it's raining heavily. When it's time for the urine tests, Newsha can't produce a sample, Niloofar isn't toilet-trained yet and we have to catch the last bus to Çankiri. I decide to urinate in all four jars.

The next week, when I take Newsha and Niloofar to the park, the air is full of smoke. The local council is pumping it out with big trucks to repel mosquitoes. Though the insects are terrible in Çankiri, using smoke to get rid of them is just as bad. The air isn't breathable, and I worry it'll make the girls ill or affect our medical tests.

The following morning there's a knock on our door. When I open it and see Barish, I feel sick with nerves. I'm sure he's found out I stole fruit from his shop.

'Kooshyar, you have a phone call,' he says.

'A phone call?' I can't believe it.

'Yes, a Dr Noori from Ankara. He wants to talk to you – he says it's important.'

Then I remember giving Barish's number to the embassy; it was the only phone number available to us. I run downstairs to his shop.

'Dr Karimi, I have the results,' says Dr Noori. 'They're all perfect, except for the urine tests,' he says. 'For some strange reason all four of them have traces of blood. If I send these results to the embassy your departure will be delayed by at least another six months. I don't think these specimens are right, though, so I want you to produce new ones. Can you all come back tomorrow?'

'Yes, of course. Thank you so much for your care.' I appreciate that Dr Noori is probably jeopardising his job by doing us this favour.

As I leave Barish's shop he yells out, 'Congratulations, Kooshyar, you're going to Australia soon!' He seems genuinely glad for me.

I thank him and go back up to our unit. I know I won't be able to get permission for us to go to Ankara tomorrow. Officer Ibtehal would love to know there's something wrong with my medical test so he can make sure I'm not able to get my application processed. I'm so anxious that I don't sleep at all that night. I realise that we have no choice: we'll have to travel to Ankara illegally.

Next morning I'm at the police station at seven-thirty, while Azita and the girls wait outside. I have my pen in my pocket, ready to sign, but I know that won't be enough to make Ibtehal happy.

He's resting his legs on top of the desk with the register, so I stand there waiting for him to move them. But he ignores me and reads his book, as usual. I notice that he's finally finished *Mouth Service* and is now reading another erotic story.

Minutes pass until finally he says from behind his book, 'What are you waiting for?'

'I wish to sign the register.'

'Sign the fucking register then!'

'I'm sorry but your legs . . .'

He pokes his head above the book and glares at me. 'Are you telling me to take my legs off the desk, you fucking refugee?' He seems particularly angry today. 'Come back later! Get out!'

If I stand up to him he might fabricate a case against me and lock me up. I walk out, frustrated and furious. We'll have to catch the next bus at eleven.

We go to the park and sit there for three hours. When we return to the police station and I go inside, a high-ranking officer is there. I gather that Ibtehal has done something wrong, and now I know why he's crankier than usual. Before signing the book I notice a rash on the senior officer's right temple, quite close to his eye. I look more closely – it doesn't seem harmless to me.

I sign the book while they keep talking. Officer Ibtehal is clearly quite fearful of the senior officer. Once I've finished, I know I should leave immediately to catch the bus – at least this time Ibtehal is too distracted to follow me – but something is bothering me.

'Excuse me, sir,' I say to the senior officer in Turkish. My language skills have improved significantly by now.

'What?' he almost yells.

'I'm a doctor – not in Turkey, of course, I have no licence to practise here, but —'

'I'm not interested in refugees' affairs,' he interrupts me.

'I'm sorry, sir, but I just wanted to let you know that the rash on your forehead looks like shingles to me.'

He touches the red spots on his temple and murmurs, 'I was probably just bitten by something last night,' before dismissing me with a wave. But as I'm stepping out of the office he asks, 'What's shingles?'

'Sir, it's a serious viral rash that can spread to the eye and cause permanent damage to your cornea. I think you should see a doctor.'

The senior officer says nothing. I leave the station and hurry with my family to catch the bus.

I drink four bottles of water on the way to Ankara. I know that a trace of blood in urine is quite common if you're dehydrated. When we arrive at Dr Noori's surgery, I go to the toilet and produce a much clearer specimen. Luckily Newsha doesn't have any problems this time, and Dr Noori helps us get a sample from Niloofar. He promises that our medical results will be ready in a few weeks.

We catch the bus home and I feel relieved. As soon as we reach Çankiri I go to the police station to sign for the afternoon, while Azita takes the girls home. Officer Ibtehal is still behind the desk, seemingly just as furious. He pretends I don't exist.

The next night we're eating our dinner of dates and bread when a knock on the door startles us. I'm worried it might be the police, coming to do another search or to check the electricity meter again, or maybe to arrest me for going to Ankara. I walk slowly to the door. 'Who is it?'

'Police.'

I open it and see the senior officer from the previous day, and I have trouble controlling my nerves. I notice a patch over his right eye.

'Dr Karimi, it's okay. I'm not going to search your house,' he says with a stern smile, then offers his hand. 'I'm here to thank you. Yesterday afternoon the rash on my forehead got worse and I remembered your warning, so I went to my doctor. He immediately sent me to hospital and they diagnosed me as having shingles. When the eye specialist applied the medication he said if I hadn't started taking it within the first seventy-two hours of getting the rash, I would've ended up with irreversible damage to my eye.'

'I'm happy you started the treatment, sir. I hope you get better soon.'

'They tell me you're going to Australia.' He smiles. 'It's a beautiful country and they're lucky to have you there.' Before he leaves he gives me his card. 'If you ever need any help, give me a call.'

When he's gone I read the card. He's Colonel Shams, Chief Commander of Police in Çankiri. I give the card to Azita for safekeeping.

A month passes – it feels longer than a century. Finally we get a letter from the Australian embassy telling us we've passed the medical test. Now we have to wait for the UNHCR and the embassy to organise visas and plane tickets, which might take another four months. Though I'm very happy we're getting closer to moving, I can't help feeling frustrated. Newsha is now six and should be at school. Any time she sees Turkish girls in their school uniforms she says to me, 'Baba jan, you told me last year I'd be going to school soon. Can I go now?' I promise her it won't be long until she's at school in Australia.

Late one afternoon, when I'm about to take the girls home from the park, Newsha insists on having one more go down the slide. I wait for her to climb up the steps and when she's sliding down I notice a man walking towards us with a little girl in his arms. It's Dariush.

'Salam, Dariush jan, how have you been?'

He shakes his head. 'Not too good. My wife . . .' He bursts into tears.

I take his daughter from him and sit her and Niloofar on the swing. While I push them gently I ask Dariush if he's had any news from the UN.

'Nothing,' he says, utterly exasperated. He picks up his daughter and they sit down on a rotten bench. It's getting dark but I can see the tears on his cheeks by the light of the only lamp in the park. His daughter has started crying too.

'She must be hungry,' I say, before immediately regretting it.

'I can't afford proper food for her,' Dariush says. I reach into my pocket and take out a five-dollar note.

'Please accept this,' I say, holding it out to Dariush.

'No, thank you. It's very kind of you but she'll be fine.'

'Please, brother, take it. We all have families – I know how hard it is. Use this to buy some milk or eggs for her, I beg you.' I push the note into his pants pocket.

Dariush looks up at me. 'Thank you,' he murmurs.

Time passes slowly and painfully. Our only relief from boredom and anxiety is through Asef and his family. Asef's situation is much worse, however: they've still not heard from the UN, and Soosan has developed severe depression. We're all really worried about her.

I keep myself busy by continuing to write my novel. I have finished the translation work but I'm also still teaching Newsha English. She's progressed a lot and now she can read simple words: Iran, Turkey, Australia, home, family, love, sister and, of course, Disneyland.

But we're increasingly finding it difficult to afford anything. Every day when I go to Barish's shop the price of bread has gone up a fraction. 'Zam,' he says, just like the fruit seller in Ankara. Today I only have five dollars, and I won't be paid for another four days.

'Just two eggs, please,' I say to Barish.

'You don't want bread today?' He raises his eyebrows.

'No.'

'Why's that?' he asks.

I feel ashamed. 'To be honest, I'm a bit short of cash this week.'

Barish silently goes to his shelves, picks up a loaf of bread and puts it on the counter. 'Take it.'

'Thank you, but I can't.'

'It's yours, please have it.' Then he adds, 'You are my neighbour.'

As I climb the stairs to our unit I hold back tears. I'm so grateful to Barish – though he's poor, he's so generous. I renew my vow to one day pay him back. I hope he never has to be a refugee, never has to experience what I've been through. That's all I can do now for this lovely, kind-hearted man: pray that he will never be in my shoes.

FOURTEEN

It's eight in the morning and I'm signing at the police station. I've noticed that Ibtehal doesn't rest his legs on the desk anymore. When I'm about to leave he tells me to wait, and then goes to the other room and comes back with a small parcel.

'Sign here and here,' he demands, showing me some forms.

'Can I ask what these are for?'

He doesn't answer and stares at me coldly, so I just quickly sign them.

When he hands me the parcel he says, 'Your passports are here, plus your visa and tickets.'

I'm so elated I smile at him. 'This doesn't mean it's over,' he says in a threatening tone, but nothing can take my joy away. I pick up the parcel and virtually run back home.

We all open the parcel together, and I show the tickets to Niloofar and Newsha.

'Look, baba! We're going to Sydney in ten days!' Niloofar smiles. She's seventeen months old now and certainly understands how wonderful this is.

'We should celebrate tonight,' I call as I go out the door. There's only forty-seven dollars in my account but I don't care anymore. In ten days I'll be a free man living in Australia. I rush to the supermarket and buy some ingredients, and this time I pay for them properly.

'We're having pizza,' I announce when I return home.

'Yay! Pizza!' Newsha shrieks happily. We haven't had it since we arrived in Turkey.

'But how are you going to cook it?' Azita asks.

'Leave it to me.'

Asef and his family join us for dinner and for the first time in months Soosan smiles. Her depression has been worsening recently but this evening, at least, she seems to be enjoying some relief.

Once Asef and I have put the ingredients on the base I place the pizza on the concrete floor, turn on the heater and hold it upside down above the food to cook it.

'This is crazy. You're going to get electrocuted,' Asef warns me.

'Don't worry, I don't die easily.'

Asef goes over to the fan to enjoy the cold wind blowing from it. 'I'm going to steal this one day soon,' he says.

That night we enjoy our wonderful pizza and some beer Asef brought. He and I stay up drinking after everyone else has gone to sleep.

'I'll miss you,' he says.

'You too. I'll do everything I can from Australia to help you,' I promise him. 'You're like a big brother to me, Asef.' I hug him. 'Please look after yourself and Soosan.'

In the morning I call Bulent from Barish's shop to give him the news and let him know when we're leaving. He's delighted. I tell him, 'I don't know how to thank you for everything you've done for me, Bulent. I wish you the best.' I say it from the bottom of my heart.

Finally our last night in Turkey arrives. Tomorrow morning we'll get on the bus for Istanbul and catch our flight to Sydney. Our Emirates airline tickets have been paid for by the UNHCR. They've told us that when we arrive in Australia, immigration officers will be waiting for us at the airport and they'll take us to our temporary accommodation.

At six o'clock I go to the police station to sign for the last time. It's meant to be Ibtehal's day off, so when I enter the office and see him behind the desk I'm surprised. I think, Maybe he's come to say goodbye to me. After I sign the book I walk towards the door.

'Where do you think you're going?' he says sarcastically. He drops something onto his desk. 'You are arrested for stealing hundreds of dollars' worth of electricity from the Turkish government.'

He must be joking. I go closer to the desk and see something that freezes every cell in my body: the broken seal of the electricity meter. I realise he must've known what I've been doing for some time but waited until the last minute to tell me. Before I can say anything, he saunters over and puts handcuffs on me.

'Ibrahim,' he yells out. 'Take this evsiz to the lockup.'

The other Turkish officer comes in and grabs my arm.

'No, you can't do this, I have a plane ticket for tomorrow, I'm under UN protection!' In less than a minute I'm locked in a windowless, concrete room. 'Let me go, please, my family are waiting for me!'

I pace up and down in my dingy cell. It's lit by a single fluorescent light and there's a small rusty metal toilet seat in a corner. I want to rip my shirt and smash the walls and scream. I bang on the big metal door and yell again but nobody answers.

Agonising hours pass by. I picture being given a jail sentence for theft and the UNHCR giving up on me. Everything I've been through and achieved over the last thirteen months in Turkey will have turned to ashes.

Suddenly there's a noise and a small panel in the door opens. 'Karimi!' cries an officer.

'Yes, yes!' I run to the door and put my hands on it.

'Your wife is here. You have two minutes.'

Azita's face appears through the panel. She looks pale and shocked. 'Kooshyar, they say they're going to take you to court tomorrow for stealing and we're going to lose our flight, our visa.' She bursts into tears.

'Listen to me, Azita. Do you remember a few months ago I gave you a business card for that colonel? Do you still have it?'

'Yes.'

'Okay, good. Call him and tell him where I am.'

'But how?'

'Go to Barish's shop. Wake him up and use his phone. Go now!'

The police officer leads Azita away. The panel shuts. I sit down and hold my head between my knees, trying to stay calm.

It's almost an hour since Azita left and I'm losing hope. What if Barish didn't let her use his phone? Or what if Colonel Shams didn't answer? Maybe he doesn't remember me – it's been months since he came to our unit.

Suddenly I hear footsteps approaching. I stand up.

'Open it!' It's the colonel's voice – a voice from heaven. When the door's unlocked I see the colonel with another officer, and Azita is behind them in tears.

'Dr Karimi, I apologise for this. You are free to go,' says the colonel.

I rush over to Azita. 'Are you okay? Where are the kids?'

'They're at Asef's house.'

I turn to the colonel and thank him profusely, shaking his powerful hand. Then we leave the station for the last time. I hurry, pushed along by the knowledge that I'll never have to see Ibtehal again.

All the way back home Azita talks about her conversation with Barish and the colonel. 'I can't believe it. We're so lucky,' she says.

First thing the next morning I go to Barish's shop to thank him. 'It's okay, Kooshyar, I'm just happy you're free now.'

'I owe you, Barish.'

'No, you don't.' Then he hands me an envelope. 'This is for you. Open it once you've left Turkey.' Surprised, I take it from him and put it in my pocket.

'Look after yourself, Barish,' I say sincerely. I turn away, knowing this is the last time I'll see this kind man.

By eight-thirty we're at the bus terminal, waiting to go to Istanbul. I'm carrying a big box and when Azita asks what it is I smile and whisper, 'It's a secret.'

Asef and his family are there with us, as is Dariush. 'What a beautiful surprise, Dariush jan,' I say when he appears. I haven't seen him for a while – I've been so worried about him.

'All the best, brother,' he says, patting me on the shoulder. He's holding his daughter with his other arm and she's smiling at me.

'What's her name?' I ask him.

'Marjan.' My heart sinks. I can't think of anything to say. 'Yes, she died last week.'

My joy at leaving Turkey evaporates. I look at the beautiful child in Dariush's arms, and I want to take her and her father with me to a better world, but I know there's nothing I can do to help them.

'Dariush jan, I'm so sorry . . .' There's a big lump in my throat. 'Please don't stay on your own – visit Asef, you need to communicate with other Iranians, you —'

'That's all right, Kooshyar jan. Enjoy your journey with your family. I just wanted to say goodbye.' He walks away and, over his shoulder, little Marjan waves to me.

Azita and Soosan are embracing and sobbing. Asef comes up to me and I snap out of my sad reverie. I promise to never forget him and to help him leave Turkey. Navid and Neema kiss Niloofar and hug Newsha. They've become close friends and this farewell is difficult even for them. I've wanted to be free for so long, but now I feel like I'm abandoning my best friend to this cruel town.

Navid says, 'Newsha, don't forget to send us letters from Australia.'

'I don't know how to write yet,' she says, 'but I'll learn soon.'

The bus arrives and passengers are told to board. I can sense a lot of Turkish people are watching us.

'The clock and the blankets and the heater are all yours, and so are the table and chairs,' I say to Asef.

'Thank you, Kooshyar jan . . . How about the fan?'

'Sorry, I had to give that to somebody else.'

He looks thoroughly dejected.

'I'm kidding. It's all yours – enjoy it.' And I hand him the big box. I've even improved the fan since he last saw it: I put a panel of hay at the front so that if you splash water on it, the air goes through the wet hay and makes it colder. It's surprisingly effective.

'Oh, thank you, Kooshyar. I can't believe it. An air conditioner, in the ugliest form imaginable.' And we both laugh.

'Don't forget to take the carpet, too,' I say. We hug for the last time.

I pick up our luggage, which contains my books, the kids' clothes, and the jar of colourful rocks. Just before we get on the bus, a red Fiat rushes into the terminal and pulls over next to us. A young couple get out: Bulent and Funda. Bulent runs over to me and grabs my arms.

'You did it, Kooshyar. You did it!'

'You're crazy. Did you drive a hundred and fifty kilometres to come here?' I ask him.

'I had to say goodbye,' he says, his large eyes shining.

I just manage to murmur, 'I'll never forget you.'

We climb on board and while the bus slowly moves out of the terminal, we look through the window at Çankiri's grey sky and the poignant farewells of our friends. I look at Asef and Bulent one more time and wave my hand. Tears course down my cheeks. The last voice I hear is Bulent's: 'I'll miss you, Pislik Yahudi!'

After a fourteen-hour trip, we arrive at Istanbul International Airport. It's colossal, with hundreds of shops packed with famous brands and high fashion. We do a lot of window-shopping, but with the knowledge we can't afford anything: we only have thirty dollars left, which we'll need in Australia. There are European tourists everywhere. For them Turkey is an easily affordable holiday destination, with beautiful beaches and mind-blowing ancient monuments. I appreciate that the country has much to offer, but not for us. The last four hundred and fifty days here as an asylum seeker, the thousands of hours waiting in agony for a visa to go somewhere safe, have felt like I've been held under the water, desperately hoping I'll be released and breathe again.

I'm about to check us in when my prepaid mobile rings for the last time. 'Kooshyar jan, are you okay?'

'Maman jan, what a lovely surprise!'

'I don't have much time, I just wanted to make sure you're fine.' I can hear she's in a hurry, and she also sounds worried.

'Yes, Maman jan. In fact, I'm happy. We're about to get on a plane and go to Australia.' Since we're so close to leaving, I figure it's now okay to tell her where we're going.

There's silence on the other end of the line. Then I hear my mother sigh, and I know she's also thinking of my brother, who moved to America while we were in Turkey. 'So far away,' she murmurs.

'Don't worry, I'll contact you regularly, Maman jan. I promise.' And she's gone.

When we board the plane I'm struck by how gigantic it is. I carefully put my hand luggage in the overhead compartment. Our seats are all together in one row, and each has a small TV screen showing a map of our route from Turkey to Australia. Newsha is thrilled.

'Baba jan, look! A map! Is that where we are?' she asks, pointing to the figure of the plane on the TV.

'Yes, Newsha. Soon we'll fly over a big ocean and in twenty-four hours, when you wake up, we'll be in Australia,' I tell her.

As we take off, my sense of relief is overwhelming. Azita looks at me, smiling broadly. 'Can you believe it, Kooshyar? We're actually going!'

I tell her I can't, and this is true. Until the last moment, even when we were inside the plane, I felt something dreadful would happen and we'd be forced to go back to Çankiri. I gaze through the small oval window at the clouds. This time, nothing has gone wrong. We've left Turkey.

Half an hour later the flight attendants start to serve refreshments. Newsha has an orange juice, and she's so excited. She hasn't had juice for more than a year. I watch her joyfully sipping it. Though she's no longer an asylum seeker, I know I have a big task in front of me. I'll have to guide her, protect her and provide for her in a new, unfamiliar country. I'll have to start over and build a new life for my family.

Suddenly I remember the envelope Barish gave me. I take it out of my pocket and open it carefully. It's a two-page letter, written in Turkish.

Dear Kooshyar,

I decided to write to you after your wife came to my shop to ring Colonel Shams. There is something I want you to know.

There are seven brothers and sisters in my family. The youngest sister is nineteen and the oldest brother thirty-one. Eight years ago my father passed away from tuberculosis. My older brother and I then started working as labourers so we could save enough money to open this grocery shop and provide for the rest of the family. Everything was fine until three years ago when my mother was diagnosed with breast cancer. We knew she'd need to have an operation and chemotherapy, and it'd be expensive. My older brother Tarkan decided to go to Europe to work so he could earn enough to pay for her treatment. He went to Germany through people smugglers and since then he's been living there as an asylum seeker, just like you. His wife and son are still in Turkey, staying with us. Tarkan has been working hard on a construction site and sending money to us. My mother had the operation and the treatment, and she was fine. We've never let her know how difficult life is for Tarkan. He rings once a month and tells me how hard he has to work and how much humiliation he has to put up with. My mother just thinks Tarkan lives happily in Germany and one day his wife and son will join him there.

Kooshyar, whenever you came to my shop and bought bread and potatoes to feed your children, you reminded me of Tarkan.

Seven months ago I woke up to a noise in my shop. I saw a shadow going through the fruit boxes. I picked up my machete and watched. The man put a few mandarins and apples in a sack. I noticed he didn't go to my till – he didn't try to take any cash. When he was about to leave I saw his face in the moonlight. It was you. I decided not to do anything because I don't want any German to hit or jail my brother if he has to steal to stop himself from starving. I just went back to sleep. After that night I knew every single time you came to my shop. I even knew which night you'd come: Thursdays!

Two months ago a police officer, Ibtehal, came to my shop and said some houses had been broken into, and he asked me if I had been robbed. I said no. He even asked about you specifically, and said he had a suspicion you were stealing from me. I told him you're a decent man and you've never tried to steal anything from me. He insisted he could jail you if I signed a report against you but I refused. I think he is cruel. Men like him should not be in charge of the Turkish police.

Unfortunately my mother passed away three months ago. Tarkan doesn't know. If I tell him he will lose heart and I want him to stay hopeful and survive, just like you. I want Tarkan to bring his wife and his little son over to Germany one day. His dream is to open a grocery shop somewhere in Cologne. I pray for him every night.

I wish you and your family the best, Kooshyar. I hope you have a great life in Australia.

Your Turkish brother,

Barish

I cannot stop the tears rolling down my cheeks. I fold Barish's letter and put it back in my pocket.

So many people have helped us over the last thirteen months: the man who gave me a bowl of rice at the beggars' house every day; the man who gave a peach to Newsha; Bulent and his mother; Habib, who let us live in his unit for free; the man who gave me his mobile phone to ring my mother; Colonel Shams; and Barish. Turkey truly has some angels. Isn't the Middle East the cradle of civilisation, the place where society began? If there were more people in the world like Barish and Bulent, there would be no starving children, no asylum seekers, no people smugglers. No need for the UNHCR.

'Baba jan, look.' Newsha pulls my sleeve and points at the TV screen. 'Iran!'

The map shows our plane flying over Iran, and all of a sudden my mind is bombarded with memories of my homeland: having pet pigeons when I was ten; the moment my friend Vahid died in front of me in the middle of the street; witnessing a dissident being hanged publicly; the day my father left us forever; going to my friend Mohsen's funeral and seeing his jacket covered with bullet holes after he was executed for joining an opposition group; the day I saw the body of another friend, Hadi, with one bullet in his chest after he was killed during his military service; my meetings with brave royalists; the agonising pain of my chest being burned with cigarettes and of my feet and back being whipped. And I remember the scent of rosewater in my mother's rice, the smell of hot, fresh bread and cardamom tea on a chilly autumn morning, and the sight of millions of red poppies after the first rain in spring. I see my brother's smiling face in front of me, congratulating me for getting excellent marks in my final school exams. 'You're going to be Dr Karimi soon!' Ah Koorosh, I think, how I wish we could've had one more meal with Maman jan in her house before we both left Iran.

And as I watch the plane crossing the Persian Gulf I murmur, 'Goodbye, my beautiful Iran.'

FIFTEEN

After a two-hour stop in Qatar and another eighteen hours of flying, we finally arrive in Sydney. When the plane lands we're all emotionally and physically exhausted. It is 20 August 2000, a few weeks before the start of the Olympic Games. I'm carrying Niloofar and dragging our luggage behind me when an airport worker approaches us. 'Let me carry that, sir.'

She's pointing at the luggage. I stare at her – it's unimaginable to me that a woman would carry something so heavy. In the Middle East men always do this for women. 'No, thank you,' I say as politely as possible.

'Okay, sir, let me get the baby, then,' she says, smiling. I've never been called 'sir' before. I gratefully hand Niloofar to her. 'She's lovely,' says the woman. Australians are friendlier than I could have hoped for.

When we emerge from Customs into the main airport we see a man carrying a sign with the UNHCR logo on it. He takes us to his car and tells us he'll drive us to the short-term unit we've been allocated in the western suburb of Auburn. On the way he mentions a few things about Australia. 'If you want to cross the road, press a button at the traffic light and wait for the green light.'

'And all the cars will then stop for us?' I ask, amazed. No one in Iran would stop for anyone crossing the road. (In 2006, 21 000 people were killed in road accidents there.) To me it's another indication of how safe, well-organised and liberated this country is.

We arrive at our two-bedroom unit in a large red brick building near the train station. It's fully furnished and when Azita opens the fridge, she exclaims with joy. There it is, just as she was told: a jug full of orange juice.

Later in the afternoon we go out to explore. However, the longer we walk around, the less impressed we are. The first thing I notice when we leave the unit is the huge mosque in Sunni-style architecture near the train station. Most women we see in the street are wearing burqas, which are rare in Iran. Hardly anyone seems to speak English – they all talk in Arabic – and every second shop is a Turkish kebab takeaway. None of this is what we expected to find in Australia.

The last UNHCR officer we saw in Turkey, who was in charge of our travel to Australia, gave us some rudimentary advice on how to begin our life here. 'The first place you should go to is Centrelink. They'll give you some money until you find a job,' he told us.

There's a Centrelink office just a hundred metres from our unit.

It's huge, with long queues and many employees. After waiting an hour I finally get to see an officer. She's very nice while she asks me to fill out a lot of forms, including one to get a tax file number. In Iran almost no one pays tax. People just bribe tax officers, as they do with the police.

Once we've finished doing the paperwork the Centrelink officer tells me, 'We'll pay you three hundred and fifty-two dollars a week for three months. After that, you'll have to find a job.' Then she asks me to go to the bank and open an account. We have very little to put into it: we stopped getting money from the UN as soon as we left Turkey.

I thank her, impressed by this country's generosity towards its poor. If you have no job and no money in Iran, the government won't help you and you die in the streets. However, I remember the woman at the Australian embassy saying it would be a long and difficult process to resume working as a doctor here. When I ask the Centrelink officer about it she tells me I have' to contact the Australian Medical Council to start the process. 'But yes, it's complicated and can take many years,' she says sympathetically.

As I walk out an Iranian-looking man in his late twenties comes up to me. 'You must be from Iran,' he says in Farsi. He introduces himself as Hossain, a common Iranian name. 'I migrated to Australia five years ago. It's hard at first but once you settle in, your life will be great,' Hossain says with a smile. Then he asks me about our accommodation and when I say I've no idea where to look or how much we should spend, he volunteers to help. He tells me that finding somewhere in Sydney won't be easy – almost impossible, in fact – because I have no rental history and no job. Then he says, 'Don't worry, though. Leave it with me.'

The next day I meet him at the bank so he can help me open an account for my Centrelink payments. I'm given an EFTPOS card, which I've never heard of. 'People here hardly carry cash – you pay with this card instead,' Hossain tells me. 'You enter a PIN number and then money is taken from your account. I'll explain it properly later on,' he assures me. Then we go to a real estate agent together. Hossain encourages me to rent a house instead of a unit because it's more comfortable, and after seeing a few old houses in Westmead I pick the cheapest one.

The application form asks for the details of my current landlord and how much rent I'm paying. Hossain puts down his name and address as my landlord and writes on the form that I work as a painter. He gives the name of a friend of his as my employer. I have to admit that without his help we'd be stranded, and I start to feel like I've found another Bulent. But instinct tells me there's something shifty about Hossain.

Three days later we move into our first home in Sydney. We have no furniture and Hossain tells me I should go to Jewish Care. I've told him a little about my Jewish heritage, which I don't usually disclose to anyone but I know I'm safe in Australia. 'Why didn't you mention this before?' Hossain asked in surprise. 'You have nothing to worry about here. Jews are very powerful and rich in Sydney.'

The next morning I leave at eight o'clock to go to Jewish Care. I take a bus and a train to get to their large building in Bondi Junction. The receptionist guides me into a room and a woman in her fifties enters shortly afterwards. Her name is Karen and she's an Ashkenazi Jew from Eastern Europe. She wants to know how many Jews live in Iran, how they live there, why I left, and what would happen if I went back.

After what reminds me of a MOIS interrogation, Karen leaves the room. I sit on my chair for several minutes, anticipating great news. When she returns, Karen's smiling and carrying a bottle of red wine. 'Here, Kooshyar, we have a nice wine from Israel for you and seventy-five dollars in cash. We wish you all the best in Australia.' And she exits the room again.

By the time I reach home I've spent fifteen dollars on public transport.

The next day, a truck stops in front of our house. It's from St Vincent de Paul, a charity run by the Catholic Church. They give us three foam mattresses, four foam pillows and a small table. The truck driver then says, 'Here's the number of a lady who has more stuff for you. She's just bought some new furniture and she wants to give her old things to a poor family. You'd better contact her.'

That night I lie on one of the mattresses and wonder at how kind the church was to give us some furniture. Later on I find out it was Jewish Care who contacted them.

The following day Hossain and I go to the kind lady's house. She lives in Turramurra, an attractive and expensive area of Sydney. She gives me a chair, a fan, a mini TV and a small fridge. I thank her sincerely and we manage to squeeze everything into Hossain's car. On our way back I notice a shop that belongs to St Vincent de Paul.

'They sell secondhand stuff,' Hossain says. 'It's all very cheap.'

I go inside and buy a beautiful black, shiny, antique typewriter for five dollars. We squeeze it between the other stuff and rush home. I start using it that same night – and so my writing career in Australia begins.

On day seven, when I have no money left, my first Centrelink payment is deposited into my bank account. I feel enormously relieved, but I want to find a job as soon as possible. Hossain introduces me to Jamal, an acquaintance of his who has a mirror shop in Sydney's pleasant North Shore area. He needs a labourer.

'What can you do?' asks Jamal.

'Everything – carpentry, mechanics, labouring, tailoring, plumbing, electronics.'

I start immediately, earning fifty dollars a day. Jamal also tells me he has a car for sale, a 1986 Holden station wagon for five hundred dollars. I haven't got that much cash but Jamal agrees to accept instalments over three months. I haven't been behind the wheel for more than a year so when I drive home I'm thrilled, even though this old Holden is not quite as nice as my luxury Peugeot in Iran. When I arrive back I don't knock on the door; I honk the horn instead. Azita and the girls climb into the car excitedly and we go for a ride. Three hours later, though, the car breaks down and we have to pay a mechanic to jumpstart it so we can return home.

The next day, when I try to pay for petrol, there's no money in my bank account. I'm shocked and embarrassed. The kind man at the petrol station agrees for me to come back and pay later, as it's only twenty dollars. It takes me just a few seconds to guess that Hossain has robbed me. When we came back from my job interview with Jamal, Hossain asked to borrow my EFTPOS card to buy cigarettes, saying he'd forgotten to bring his wallet. I could not refuse him because of our cultural background, so I gave him my PIN and stayed in his car while he cheated me. He knew very well how to deceive an Iranian newcomer.

Neither Jamal nor I see Hossain again. I presume he's gone to a different Centrelink to prey on another newly arrived Iranian. What he's done doesn't make me angry. It just saddens me profoundly.

We start to feel settled and life falls into a routine but I don't want to work at Jamal's shop forever. I aspire to use my real expertise in medicine and authorship. My biggest passion in life, writing, is still intact but there's absolutely no hope I'll be able to write professionally in English. I try to improve my language skills by watching SBS and reading the subtitles. I also start typing up my story, working late at night. When Azita discovers me at the typewriter and I tell her what I'm doing, she's horrified.

'No! No way are you doing that. If you write our story I'll divorce you and go straight back to Iran with the kids. We've had enough.' Azita already knows that under Australian law she is free to divorce me, unlike Iranian law.

'But I have to show people what we've been through. It's not just about us – thousands have been jailed and tortured and executed by the regime,' I point out.

'I said *no*.' And she slams the door.

I have only two options: forget about writing or do it in secret. But I can't forget about writing. It wasn't Azita who was kidnapped and barbarically tortured and forced to cooperate with an evil system. So I write only when she's asleep, and lie to her when she finds me out of bed at night. I can't stay silent and let the Islamic killing machine continue to function. I don't care about the dangers – I've seen what's behind Iran's veil and have to reveal it to the world.

As I'm leaving Jamal's shop one day, my mobile phone rings. There's no caller ID so I assume it's my mother. We speak once a month and although our conversations are always coded, because her phone is tapped, it's reassuring just to hear her voice.

'Salam, Kooshyar jan,' a man says. I can't identify him, though he sounds familiar.

'Salam. Who is this?' I ask in Farsi.

After a long pause the voice says, 'It's me, Haji Heydar.' I'm taken aback: I haven't heard from him in almost two years. But I've known him for much longer than that. When I was nine my mother secretly arranged a *sigha* and became his temporary wife. In an Islamic version of prostitution, a woman can be married to a man for an agreed period of time, ranging from a few hours to several years, the terms being agreed by both parties. This kind of deal is quite common and entirely legal; married men can organise as many *sigha* as they want. All they have to do is pay a fee, which in my mother's case was ten dollars a fortnight. To feed us, my mother gave her body to this man, a devout bourgeois Muslim with a wife and family. Now, Haji Heydar stays with his wife full-time and has stopped visiting my mother.

'I'm not very well,' he tells me. 'I had a second heart attack, and the doctors say I don't have much time left.'

I find it difficult to sympathise with this man. He'd come to our house every lunchtime and sit on our one fancy chair to eat his kebab with special bread and gulp his juice, while my mother, Koorosh and I sat on the floor and ate eggs and stale bread. As soon as I left Iran he ditched my mother and didn't return her phone calls asking for help.

'Kooshyar, I know we'll never see each other again so I've called you to say something very important.' Haji takes a deep breath. 'I want you to forgive me.'

I realise how hard it is for a proud and powerful man like Haji Heydar to say these words. But I also know that as a devout Muslim he wants to enter paradise, and he won't be able to unless he's pardoned by the people he wronged. I wonder how large Haji's telephone bill will be this month after he's asked everyone for forgiveness.

'Haji, there's nothing to forgive. I don't have any hard feelings against you. I wish you the best,' I murmur, struggling to mean what I say. Nevertheless one thing has altered inside my heart. I feel less hatred for Haji than I do for the system that enabled his behaviour.

'May Allah protect you, son,' he says and hangs up – afraid, no doubt, I might change my mind if he says anything else. There was no love between Haji and my mother. She satisfied him sexually and thereby boosted his ego, but she hated him. Haji let her collect his breadcrumbs to feed her malnourished boys. I loved and admired my mother for everything she gave me. How could I not? But Haji owned her. That's also why I went to medical school, asides from my promise to my mother to help the people in the slums: I had to become a doctor to buy her back, to make sure she no longer needed to depend on this evil man who was using her as his sex slave. And I did.

This is the last time I hear from Haji Heydar. A month later he suffers a cardiac arrest in hospital and dies. By this time I've truly forgiven him, realising that it's more important to focus on making Iran a more equal and tolerant civilisation than harbour vengeful thoughts about people like him.

Working for Jamal turns out to be awful. When he discovers I was a doctor in Iran he becomes condescending and refuses to believe I was financially comfortable there. I seem to be paying for him being degraded by the rich and successful back home. I try hard to prove to him I don't care about people's social position or their financial status and tell him about growing up in poverty, but nothing makes him be friendlier towards me.

Not long after I've started there, I learn that the lowest labourers' wage should be seventy dollars for an eight-hour day. I work eleven- or twelve-hour days, sometimes more, for just fifty dollars. A week later the car breaks down again and the mechanic tells me it's worth less than a hundred dollars. I have to leave it with him for a month while I save seven hundred dollars to get it fixed. Jamal even blames me for the car's failure.

'You don't know how to drive a car like this. It's probably the first time you've even owned a car.' I don't bother correcting him. The minds of men like Jamal and Ibtehal are trapped inside a pingpong ball, with only a pinhole to see the real world.

I decide to focus on qualifying as a doctor in Australia. When I contact the Australian Medical Council they tell me I'll have to sit an English exam first, then a written exam, and then a clinical exam. Each takes place six to twelve months after the previous one, which means that even if I pass all of them on the first try, I won't get a medical licence for at least two years. When I do, I'll then have to work another twelve months as an intern in a public hospital outside Sydney on a minimal salary.

'I'm not going to do this. It's ridiculous!' I say to Azita. I under-stand the need for exams, but why over such a long period? On top of this, there are no training courses and we're not allowed to go to a hospital or clinic and observe the way doctors practise here, so it's likely that by the time I sit the final exam I'll have lost a lot of my knowledge and skills. How can I study dozens of huge medical textbooks when I have to work at Jamal's shop to survive? It seems to me they'd rather refugees install mirrors in toilets than practise medicine. And yet they say in the news all the time they need doctors and nurses.

The next day Jamal notices my frustration and asks me what's going on. When I tell him about how difficult it is to practise medicine here, his reaction is predictable. 'I've met many doctors and engineers from Iran in Sydney – they all drive cabs here.' He grins at me. 'You're lucky you have this job. You have no idea how many guys wanted to work for me. I decided to give the job to you because you have a family to feed. I felt sorry for your kids.'

I say nothing to Jamal, remembering my father's advice: 'The best response to idiots is silence.'

I go home, hold my Star of David and vow to become a doctor in Australia, even if it takes ten years. I want to become a proud citizen of this country and support those who need help. This time, I will practise medicine to buy back my self and my pride, and the dignity of my family.

I ring my father that night. I miss him and need to hear his voice. When we finish our short conversation he asks me how the weather is in Germany. His oldest son from his first wife was one of Iran's top students and went to Germany on a scholarship, so if anyone leaves the country my father thinks they must be in Germany. His universe is very simple, just like his bus: there's Iran, there's the sun, there's the moon, and there's Germany. I don't try to explain that I'm in Australia. Then he says, 'God be with you, Koorosh.' I'm not surprised he calls me by my brother's name, but it makes me wonder if he cares about me at all. I've never been able to work it out.

Fifty dollars a day doesn't cover the costs of a family of four so I start doing deliveries for a pizza shop near home as well. I work there from seven till ten-thirty, and make around thirty dollars a night.

Now, after working in the mirror shop during the day and the pizza shop in the evening, I come home and study and then, well after midnight, keep writing my story. Years of loveless marriage have made me an expert in concealment; I could launch a missile from our kitchen without Azita suspecting anything. I have no hope that my manuscript will be published. I write a page and tear it up – it's no good. Though I was a respected writer and translator in Iran, English is not my mother tongue and writing in a foreign language is like painting with no arms. I'm only smudging the canvas now, but I won't give up. I refuse to give up.

Newsha has started at Parramatta North Public School. Her first few months are heartbreaking. She doesn't understand what people are saying, and they can't understand her. Every day she comes home crying and we keep encouraging her to continue trying to find friends, to understand the teacher, to speak with others. After three months, amazingly, she starts speaking English. It's unbelievable how fast children can learn a language. After one year her English far surpasses mine, and when I try to speak it she laughs and corrects me. I feel delightfully mocked – nothing is more pleasant in life than your child surprising you with her intelligence.

Six months pass and we're sitting at home watching the news when Asef calls. In the last few months whenever we've spoken he's been deeply depressed, struggling to remain hopeful. Now, though, he's full of excitement.

'Guess what? We got the fax!' Finally, after more than two years, the UNHCR has accepted his case. I tell him to request to be sent to Australia, and he agrees. 'That would be amazing! I'll keep my fingers crossed.'

I ask him about Dariush, and he's silent for a moment. Then he tells me that the UNHCR rejected Dariush's case and he's disappeared. There were rumours that after losing all hope he wrote a letter, held his daughter close to his chest and jumped into the river. The Turkish police seem to have covered up the story but a friend of Dariush's, who has the letter, is appealing to the UN. I'm speechless, utterly devastated. The joy at Asef's great news disappears like a crystal dropped into quicksand. I think, Who is responsible for this? Why do such things happen?

I search the streets every Friday night for abandoned goods. I find a broken iron and a dead microwave, and fix them at home. We go to the Salvation Army one day and they give us a used pram for Niloofar, as well as a cup of coffee and a sandwich.

After seven months in Australia, Newsha and Niloofar finally have beds. I found them by the side of the road and repaired them, but we can't afford proper mattresses so the girls still sleep on foam ones. Azita and I sleep on the floor until I collect some timber and make a bed. My carpentry skills haven't improved since Çankiri but this time – thank God – I don't catch influenza. The bed is very unstable but it's better than nothing. We use it for two and a half years until I manage to buy a brand-new one.

After eight months I pass my first exam, the occupational English test. Now I can apply to sit the written medical exam, a difficult test requiring eight years' worth of knowledge to be squeezed into three hundred complicated questions. Many overseas doctors fail this exam the first or even the second time they take it, and it's expensive: twelve hundred dollars. I have to wait for another eight months before I can do the test in Sydney.

I'm beginning to see many possibilities for our new life, but Azita is not. Almost every time I come home from work I find her in tears. One night she is completely without hope.

'I want to go back to Iran, Kooshyar,' she says. 'I can't do this anymore. We've lost all our friends and family, our homeland, our identity, and now we have nothing. You'll be a labourer and a pizza-delivery man forever. Everything we own is secondhand or broken. At least in Turkey we had hope – we thought we were going to a wonderful place – but look at us! We're nobodies here.'

I gently tell her she can't go back to Iran, not now. We're a family and we've stayed together; we survived Turkey so we can get through this. We'll eventually find friends and have a better life. I don't know how much I believe this myself but I'm trying to reassure her. At least as a doctor I know how to give hope, even if there is none, but my situation is not much better than Azita's. Every morning I wake up with a splitting headache after terrible nightmares. I dream I'm in jail being tortured by the intelligence service, or I see myself being chased through the streets of Tehran by the secret police, and at the end I'm always killed. I never tell Azita about these nightmares and flashbacks. I have to pretend to be happy and hopeful because my family needs me – in this foreign, faraway country, I'm all they have.

So I promise Azita that our future will be great. I promise I'll pass the exams. I suggest she should study or find a job, hoping this will distract her and give her and our family some social life.

Azita thinks about my words and a week later tells me she's registered at TAFE to study hairdressing part-time.

'Are you sure about this?' I ask.

'Yes, I love hairdressing,' she says excitedly. 'It's in my blood.' She's right: we know many Iranian women who became hairdressers and beauticians when they moved to Australia. I wonder if being free of harsh restrictions on their appearance stirs in these women an intense, impulsive love of beauty and style; some might even say they develop an obsession with it.

Six months later Azita begins working as an apprentice at a salon owned by another Iranian woman. Mary is kind and treats Azita with respect, and soon we become friends with her and her husband, Ben. In England he did a PhD in textiles but he couldn't find a job in that industry in Australia, so he manages their other hairdressing salon.

By this time we've also become close with a lovely Iranian family: Saman, his wife Shohreh and their children. Their daughter goes to the same school as Newsha, though she is three years ahead of her. They've been living in Australia for more than ten years and share their experiences with us. We go to their house as often as possible – emotional isolation is the hardest part of our life here. Saman was originally an accountant but he's working as a painter in Sydney because he couldn't get his qualifications recognised. He confirms I'm being significantly underpaid by Jamal but unfortunately there's no job available where Saman works.

As the date for my written exam approaches, I stay up late every night studying after delivering pizzas. I'm always tired; Jamal is making me work more than usual. I've mastered mirror cutting, sandblasting, mirror tiling, framing and installation, and he wants to employ me permanently.

'I want to open a new branch in Parramatta and get you to run it. Forget about medicine. I know you won't pass the exams – this is not like Iran,' he says to me.

'I'm going to try,' I tell him as I sandblast a big shower screen, carving a large mermaid on it for the wealthy man who's ordered it.

His tone changes back to its usual level of aggression. 'I've noticed you reading medical books at work. You're not allowed to bring books here anymore.'

'But I only study between jobs.'

'This is a workplace. If you want to study, don't come to work.'

So I can no longer study at work. Jamal's bitterness is catching.

It's the day before the exam, which will be in the south-eastern suburb of Maroubra. Because I don't trust my car to last the distance I decide to catch public transport there, but I only have five dollars in my pocket and nothing left in my poor bank account. I ask Jamal to advance my next pay but he refuses. I'll have to borrow money from someone and the only friend I have is Saman.

At eight that night I tell Azita I'm going out for a walk, and go over to Saman's house. When he answers the door he assumes I'm there because I'm anxious about the exam, so he brings me inside to have a chat and give me courage and hope. At the end of our conversation I thank him and he sees me out. I'm too embarrassed to tell him why I've really come. But while I'm standing out on the street, trying to work out what to do, I realise I have no choice so I knock on his door once more. Saman is surprised to see me again.

'Saman jan, I'm so sorry, I don't know how to tell you this . . . I don't have enough money to get to Maroubra for my exam tomorrow.

I was wondering if I could borrow ten dollars from you, just for a few days.'

'Why didn't you tell me before?' Saman says. He takes out his wallet and hands me a fifty-dollar note. When I protest he says, 'Kooshyar jan, please keep it. Don't worry, it's all fine.'

All the way back home I pray to Adonai to help me pass the exam. I barely sleep that night. If I fail I'll have to wait another year to resit it, but I don't know if I can find the strength or commitment to try again. I think, This is my one chance, my first and last attempt to scale this mountain. I vow that if I pass I'll help poor and desperate people and will try my best to save lives. I want to pay my debt to Australia. I remind myself that I've never failed an exam before, but I'm still apprehensive.

The exam goes for three hours and it's very intense. I face several intricate cases, many complicated scenarios and some very difficult questions. When the final bell goes we all take a deep breath. The Indian man sitting next to me looks at me in despair. 'It was horrible,' he says. I nod in silent agreement. I'm sure I've failed.

Four weeks pass in dread, with either insomnia or nightmares every night. Then a white envelope appears in the mailbox. I don't have the courage to open it, so I give it to Azita and she does it. Then she screams.

I've passed. I've climbed the first cliff.

SIXTEEN

I'm having a bad day. Jamal is furious because I spoke to a potential customer and failed to get their business. He never allows me to answer the phone; I'm 'not a smart businessman'. He's quite right, in fact. Then, because I finished late at the mirror shop, the pizza-store owner verbally abuses me too. My final delivery for the night is to a nice house in Carlingford. I ring the bell on the fancy wooden door and hear party noises from inside. A pleasant-looking man soon appears and takes the pizzas, and he puts a two-dollar coin in my hand as a tip. I walk to my car and open my hand to look at the petite coin. Here I am, on this cold winter night in Sydney, with two dollars in my hand and nothing else – no real job, no support and, worst of all, no future. My life in Australia is a vicious cycle of pointless acts. Am I going to be a lousy delivery man forever? Or a lousy mirror man forever? I need a miracle. Where's my Adonai?

When I pick up Azita from the salon the following afternoon Ben asks, 'Kooshyar, are you still working in that horrible mirror shop?'

'Yes.'

'Listen, I have an idea for you. Why don't you do body piercing? It's a booming business.'

I reject the idea immediately. There's no body piercing in Iran so I'm not familiar with it.

'You're a doctor – it should be a piece of cake for you,' he says. 'Anyway, think about it. If you decide to try it you can start any time at my hairdressing salon. It's in Parramatta at the Westfield shopping centre.'

The next day, I go to work in Jamal's mirror shop and a man in his sixties comes in carrying an old wine bottle.

'I was wondering if you can cut a small hole in the side of this. I want to put a bird in the bottle and hang it in my shop,' he says. He tells us his name is James.

Jamal inspects it. 'I'm afraid it's not possible. As soon as I put the cutter in place the bottle will shatter.'

But James insists. 'I've asked so many glass experts but they've all declined. I'm happy to pay any money for this.' Jamal shakes his head.

'I think I can do it,' I say from the corner of the shop.

'No, I don't think that's a good idea,' warns Jamal.

'How're you going to do it?' James asks.

'If you want a round hole in the bottle, I'll do it for you,' I say confidently.

'Okay, I'll let you try,' says James, handing me the dark brown bottle. 'But if you break it you'll have to give me two hundred dollars because the bottle's an antique. If you do manage to make a nice big round hole in it, I'll give you two hundred dollars.'

After he leaves Jamal is furious. 'How the hell are you going to do that?'

'I can't tell you, sorry.'

'Fine, it's your problem, I don't care. But if you make that customer angry I'll sack you.'

As soon as Jamal goes out I start the job. I'm not going to use a glass cutter. I've noticed while sandblasting that if you keep the gun on the same spot it creates a dent in the glass, so I'm hoping to do this with the bottle until I create a hole.

I draw a large circle on the bottle and cover the rest of it with masking tape. Then I put the bottle inside the sandblasting machine and secure it with more tape. I start blasting a small point on the bottle with sharp sand grains and after five minutes a small hole appears in the bottle. I'm excited – it's working. After thirty minutes I've created a perfect round and smooth hole on the side of the wine bottle.

The next morning I tell Jamal to ring James because his bottle is ready.

'Show me,' Jamal demands. He examines it. 'How did you do it?'

'With the sandblasting gun.' He walks away scowling.

In the afternoon James comes back and I hand him the bottle. He holds it and runs his finger around the edge of the hole. 'Wow! I'm impressed. Well done.'

He hands me two green hundred-dollar notes. Jamal watches in silence.

'How long have you been working in this business? I asked many experts, who've spent their whole life cutting glass, and they couldn't do it,' says James. 'Thank you.'

After he leaves, we go back to work. Later in the afternoon Jamal takes me to the house of an Iranian woman. As soon as we step inside I notice a black grand piano in a corner. We go to her bathroom and install a large mirror and shower screen. It's a big job and when I look at my watch it's seven and I'm due at the pizza shop.

'Jamal, I have to go soon to deliver pizzas.'

'Look, mate, you're working for me and you have to stay and finish this job. I don't give a fuck about your pizza delivery.' He's been cranky all day, particularly since James left.

I stay and we finish an hour later. We go back to the living room and Jamal negotiates a price with the Iranian lady. He always rips his customers off and charges more than he's quoted, but somehow he convinces them to pay. While they're talking I run my fingers over the piano keys and softly play a simple melody. All my life I've dreamed of owning a piano. I taught myself keyboard ages ago in Iran and I love listening to a song and then trying to play it.

'That's lovely,' says the Persian woman. She stops talking to Jamal and comes over to me. 'No, don't stop. Please have a seat and keep going.'

I sit down on the stool. This is the first time I've been so close to a grand piano. I start playing an old Persian love song.

'Oh my God, I haven't heard that song for twenty years. It brings back so many memories.' The woman has tears in her eyes.

Before we leave, her husband comes down from upstairs. 'So, you're a musician working as a mirror installer?' he asks.

'No, I'm just doing this temporarily,' I say.

'Please come back sometime and have dinner with us and play

the piano,' says his wife.

Before we leave she gives me a twenty-dollar tip. When we reach the shop Jamal turns to me, his face dark with anger. 'I think you should stick to delivering pizzas. The mirror business isn't good enough for you,' he says.

'But I —'

'No, that's it, mate. Goodbye.'

In the morning I go to Ben's salon in Parramatta.

'Is the offer still there?' I ask him.

'Sure is.' He smiles.

After an hour's training by another body piercer I start working at Ben's shop, called Catwalk. The next week he puts a sign out the front saying *Body Piercing By Doctor*.

'But I'm not a doctor in Australia yet,' I say nervously.

'You *are* a doctor, Kooshyar. Now we just wait for customers.' He's confident we'll be swamped with clients, and he's right. Ben is a natural-born businessman. In three weeks I'm earning between two and three hundred dollars a day, and this is only thirty percent of what I make. Ben takes the other seventy percent – he's ripping me off, but he's much nicer than Jamal. Plus he allows me to study my medical books between clients. Many people come to me because I'm a doctor. I understand human anatomy so I know where to pierce, including parts of the body that other piercers are hesitant to touch.

Two months after I start, a woman covered in piercings and tattoos comes to Ben's shop and starts yelling at us. 'This is my suburb. I've been piercing here for five years. You and your fuck'n Irani doctor should just fuck off!'

After she leaves Ben turns to me. 'Are you scared?'

'No!' I find it hilarious.

The next week a health officer from the local council comes to the salon to make sure our facilities meet their standards. It's obvious she's there because she received a complaint but she's impressed when I explain to her that, as well as using sterile packs and instruments, I'm using sterile gloves instead of disposable ones. I know about the autoclave and sterile procedures and I explain that many clients come to us because we treat the infected piercings done by others. The officer leaves and never comes back. The following week, though, Ben finds his car completely trashed. The bikie boyfriend of the rival body piercer then turns up with her at the salon and threatens to get rid of us, but when we don't show any fear they both go away.

Because my body-piercing business is going well and I no longer need a second job, I have a bit more time to study at night. When I passed the second stage of qualifying to be a doctor, with excellent results, I received a letter from the Australian Medical Council telling me I can sit for the clinical exam, the final one, in August 2002 in Melbourne.

Azita's learning fast as an apprentice for Mary and she's much less depressed these days. Life is getting easier – except for our finances, which are far from adequate. But at least I've started to see light at the end of the tunnel.

Having paid the two and a half thousand dollar exam fee, I head to Melbourne for the clinical exam. I study all night as the train rumbles its way south. This exam doesn't just test medical theory; I'll have to communicate with mock patients, examine them and make a diagnosis, as well as come up with a proper management and treatment plan. I go to the Royal Melbourne Hospital, where there are many doctors from different countries, all as nervous as I am. Some of them have been trying to pass these exams for eight years, and the more I talk to them the more disheartened I become.

Eventually the process is explained to us. There are fourteen rooms, each with a patient and one or two examiners. We're to go to each room in turn and spend five to ten minutes talking to the patient, examining them, diagnosing the disease and then explaining their treatment plan. If we don't communicate or deliver bad news properly, or calm down an angry patient, or if we make a mistake in diagnosis, we will fail. We'll receive our results in two weeks.

I'm the third doctor to begin. I try hard to stay calm and focused but some cases are quite confusing. My future is on the line again, and I'm reminded of my interview at the UNHCR in Turkey. I've told Azita that if I fail the exam I won't resit it. I've also promised Ben that if I fail we'll open a tattoo and piercing business in Parramatta. That industry is much more lucrative and less stressful than medicine, but I'm in Australia to be a doctor and save lives, to help the less fortunate.

I start at nine in the morning and finish at two, feeling exhausted, disappointed, and even more nervous. All night at my small South Melbourne motel I'm not able to sleep. I go over and over the cases and my answers. When I arrive home the following evening I tell Azita I'm certain I've failed, but she decides I'm being overly dramatic. 'You're always a perfectionist. I think you've passed,' she says. I let her stay hopeful.

At work the next day, Ben encourages me to try a tattoo course. 'Your drawing skills are excellent – you'll make a perfect tattoo artist. Do you have any idea how much money you could make? Forget about medicine. Look at me, I have a PhD in textiles but I'm so happy running this business.'

Fourteen days pass in agonising anticipation and apprehension. Every day I go over the questions and try to remember my answers, and I get more and more despondent. On the day the results are due I'm at work, piercing a girl's belly button. She's saved up to get a third piercing on her umbilicus in a triangle shape and I'm concentrating hard to get it right.

'You have a phone call,' says Kelly, one of the hairdressers. 'It's your wife.'

'I'm busy,' I reply, and the girl screams with pain when I pierce her belly button.

'She says it's important.'

'Hang on.' I thread the ring in the girl's belly button and say, 'That's it, all done. It looks gorgeous.' Kelly hands me the phone. 'Azita, what's up?'

'You passed! Kooshyar, you passed! You're a doctor!' she says, shrieking with joy.

Kelly and another hairdresser, Emily, congratulate me but Ben is less than delighted. 'So we're not going to open the shop, I'm guessing,' he says.

The next month I get my Australian medical licence. It's my greatest achievement since coming to Australia, but I can only work as a doctor in the metropolitan area after I've done my internship. Before then I'll have to practise in the country. This doesn't make much sense to me. What's the difference between sick people in the country and sick people in the city?

I decide to do my internship and am sent to St George Hospital in Sydney's southern suburbs, more than an hour from where we're living. My first days are terrible. I'm ten years older than all the other interns and I did an internship when I was their age, back in Iran, so the whole experience is humiliating. But it's unavoidable and after a few months at least I'm familiar with the routine and the system.

As part of the training I'm sent to Emergency for three months, and I love it. I decide to do it for another three months but I have to go to Sutherland Hospital instead, another forty-five minutes away. The pay is low so I start working nights as well, and interns from other wards also approach me to do their shifts. Soon I'm hardly seeing my family and many mornings I almost fall asleep driving home. Even worse, though, is the discrimination at the hospital. Some of the staff look down on overseas-trained doctors, especially when the language barrier causes problems, and their judgemental treatment and hostility can make life unpleasant. Regardless of how well we do we're still stigmatised as OTDs, and sometimes I feel so frustrated and angry I want to scream. It's like banging your head against a wall.

One of the senior doctors at Sutherland is a very difficult man. Whenever it's time for handover he talks to all the other doctors but not me. Any time I double-check a treatment or ask him for a second opinion he looks at me irately, sighs in frustration and says something like, 'I'm busy now,' or, 'I can't help you – go ask someone else.' I don't understand why Dr Gordon seems to hate me so much.

One evening I'm treating Joshua, a ten-year-old boy who's had a skateboard accident and suffered a laceration on his right leg. I explain to his parents and grandmother that I'll give Joshua some laughing gas to ease the pain, and then I'll inject a small amount of local anaesthetic to numb the wound before putting in a few stitches. They seem happy with this and Joshua is quite cooperative and brave. I give him the injection and begin inserting the sutures into the wound. The second part is extremely easy for me; I've repaired extra-thin hymen membranes.

'What's going on here?' Dr Gordon is suddenly behind me. He grabs the needle. 'We don't suture kids in Australia like this,' he says, and takes over my work. I feel embarrassed in front of Joshua's family and walk over to another patient nearby. I surreptitiously watch Dr Gordon give Joshua more local anaesthetic and wonder why he's done this. Joshua clearly doesn't like the extra needle. I then keep myself busy with the other patient, who has presented with chest pain.

Half an hour later, while I'm inserting a cannula into a patient's hand, someone calls out to me. I turn around and see Joshua's grandmother coming towards me.

'Is Joshua okay?' I ask.

'Yes, Doctor, he's fine. I just wanted to say thank you. That arrogant doctor who interrupted you was incredibly rude. I don't know why he gave Joshua more anaesthetic – you'd already done an excellent job.'

'Thank you, ma'am.' I smile back at her and she pats me on my shoulder and walks away. Her kind touch restores my faith in Australians and gives me confidence. I won't give up!

When my twelve-month internship finishes, the Australian Medical Council tells me I have to work for *ten years* in rural Australia before I'm able to practise in the city. This is a new rule specifically for OTDs. How can I take my children to a remote town where they won't know anyone? They've only just found friends and a social life in Sydney, and Azita has started to feel comfortable here and is even planning to open her own hairdressing salon. My only alternative is to work as a locum in hospitals around Sydney and the surrounding towns. I hate doing this but I have no choice, so I begin work as an Emergency locum. One day I'm at the Prince of Wales Hospital in Randwick, the next at Blacktown Hospital, the day after that at Lithgow Hospital, and so on. Some places are an hour's drive away, some three hours'. At least the pay is good.

I'm at Manly Hospital at one in the morning when an ambulance brings in a good-looking young man on a stretcher. He seems quite distressed and is perspiring profusely. When I ask him what's wrong he talks quickly in a strong Australian accent, using slang terms I don't understand. All I can get from him is: 'I was at home playing with kids . . . toy car . . . went to my . . . very painful . . .' I'm trying hard to comprehend what he's saying but without success.

Dr Barlow, the head of the department, sees my confusion and comes over to help. I explain that I don't know what's happened to this patient. 'Okay, let me have a chat with him,' he offers.

A few minutes later he comes back to me, smiling. 'I can explain the problem,' he says. 'He was having sex with another man and they used a sex toy, which is like a probe, and it went in too far and has actually ruptured his rectum. He has an ischiorectal abscess which, as you know, is very serious so I'm sending him straight to theatre.'

I'm so embarrassed for not understanding the patient straight away. 'I'm very sorry.'

'No, no! It's just a language barrier – it has nothing to do with your medical knowledge. I know you're a competent doctor.'

After that I make sure I listen very carefully to my patients. If

I don't understand something I ask again, often several times. But I don't mistake a sex toy for a car anymore.

One night in late summer I'm at home when I get a phone call from Iran. It's Parvin, Dad's second wife, who burned me when I was a child. Later on she told me that Abraham, my mother's uncle, paid her to do this. He didn't want to have a half-Muslim relative.

'I'm sick of your father,' Parvin tells me. 'He's seventy-eight years old and can't work anymore, and I'm not going to look after him at my house. If one of his kids doesn't help me I'll throw him out onto the street to die.' When my father retired as a bus driver at age seventy he became a taxi driver in Tehran. Three years ago he stopped doing that and took a job as a receptionist in a driving agency, until they finally sacked him because he was too frail.

There are no nursing homes for poor people in Iran. If Parvin carries out her threat, my father will only last a few days. Inexplicably, she was always his favourite wife out of the three – he bought her a house and supported her all her life. I can't let her abandon him in his old age; after all, I still love my father.

Parvin says Koorosh can't afford to help and my stepbrothers from my father's first wife – one lives in Germany and the other in Tehran – have refused to assist because he neglected them.

'Parvin, don't worry, just tell me how much you need.'

'Two hundred and fifty dollars a month.'

'Okay, I'll send that amount every month, I promise.'

'Thank you, Kooshyar, thank you so much. I always knew the youngest would be the best son. I wish you were still in Iran.' She suddenly sounds so kind, polite and happy.

I explain the situation to Azita and she's outraged. 'But this is the vicious woman who tried to kill you! She'll probably just spend the money on herself and her daughter. Besides, that man never cared for you. Remember how when we got married, and then when we had Newsha, he didn't even bother to call? Does he even know where you live?' In the end she grudgingly accepts me just sending money for three months, but I continue doing it for some years. I believe it's my responsibility as a son to protect my father, even if he doesn't know where I live.

Because I'm working long hours as a locum every day, my income increases significantly. I purchase a nicer car and we finally get a proper bed, decent furniture, and new kitchen appliances and clothes.

'We have to buy a house, Kooshyar. We can't rent forever and our new furniture looks horrible in this awful place,' Azita says.

So I work even harder – night and day, seven days a week. By the time I get home it's usually three-thirty in the morning and everyone's asleep. In February 2004 I manage to buy an old four-bedroom brick house in Baulkham Hills, north-west of Sydney, from a retired Iranian man who used to be a doctor. He failed the AMC exams twelve times so, after several years of driving a taxi, he instead opened a flower shop with his wife. The following month we move into the first house we own in Sydney. It's delightful seeing my family so full of hope and happiness. But sadly this joy doesn't last.

Azita wants to have her own hairdressing salon, so I borrow from the bank to set her up in the western suburb of Quakers Hill. The business does well and a few years later she owns another two salons. I'm working in more and more remote towns and am hardly at home. I miss my daughters, the little girls we brought to Australia after so much suffering and struggle. Newsha's now fourteen and

Niloofar's eight. Though Azita finally has the material success she's always wanted, I don't find this satisfying. While I'm sleeping on spring beds in Emergency rooms, Azita's driving her new Mercedes to nightclubs and restaurants with her good-looking friends. I'm a senior medical officer now and have saved many lives, but I'm lonelier than ever. I can feel things are slowly but undeniably slipping away from me.

SEVENTEEN

It's 2009 and Azita's salons are not doing well. Over the last nine months we've spent a lot of time and money trying to attract customers and improve the businesses. Then early one morning I come home to find Newsha crying in her room. When I ask her what's wrong, she shares her true feelings with me for the first time in ages. It tears at my heart when she says she's hardly seen me or her mother over the last three years. She tells me that Niloofar suffers from nightmares and almost every night gets up and goes to Newsha's room for comfort.

I'm speechless. Newsha's words put everything I've done under a gigantic question mark. What have I really achieved in Australia? A luxury car and a house, credit card debts and business loans, and a dysfunctional family? Am I saving lives in Emergency rooms while my own children are fading away? I feel as if I'm sitting in a broken boat, watching them drowning silently.

I virtually beg Azita to drop two of the salons and just keep one of them. At first she refuses, arguing that they're new businesses and need time, but eventually she agrees and we close them down.

It's five years since I began working as a locum in hospitals across New South Wales: Dubbo, Parkes, Forbes, Lithgow, Mudgee, Maitland, Wellington and Cowra, as well as all over Sydney. I know how to resuscitate a cardiac patient and often have to work as a cardiologist, surgeon, obstetrician or orthopaedic registrar, as there's usually no specialist support in rural towns. I've been offered permanent jobs in many of these places but I need to stay in the city for my family. The question is: Do I still have a family?

When I return home after three months of working day and night in Parkes, Azita tells me she wants to speak with me.

'Kooshyar, I don't think I can live with you anymore. You and I have been through a great deal together but I don't love you, and I know you feel the same way. I want to find love before it's too late.'

What can I say? My wife has already taken off her wedding ring. It's too late for anything. Thursday 22 April 2010 becomes one of the saddest nights of my life.

I pick up my jacket and walk out of the house. I end up giving Azita almost everything I've bought during our ten years in Australia – the cars, the salon, the house, the furniture – except for my piano. The girls are devastated and I feel extremely guilty. I've always promised to care for and protect them, and now I feel like I'm deserting them. My heart bleeds for my daughters every minute of every day. Though our marriage had its problems I never wanted to divorce Azita, mostly because of my parents' situation and the damage caused by my father's absences. I curse my destiny for letting my family fall apart after everything we've sacrificed, everything we've endured. The pain is worse than that inflicted by my MOIS torturers. They only managed to break my skull, this has broken my back.

I begin to think constantly of suicide. Every time I build up my life from scratch, something always shatters it to pieces. But I'm not allowed to die; I can't end my misery. How can I leave my innocent, traumatised daughters without a father to listen to them when they're crying with loneliness and despair? And what about my promise to my mother when I was dying from typhoid? Or my vow to my Adonai?

One morning I get up, take a deep breath, clutch my Star of David and start picking up the pieces. I move to Tea Gardens, a small coastal town near Newcastle, and work six days a week as a GP specialising in skin cancer. I go to Sydney every weekend to see my children and support them and their mother. Still, the girls are slipping towards major depression.

I love the work I'm doing and soon I love the community, which is full of exceptionally kind people, many of whom form a special bond with me. I also keep myself busy writing, finishing the eleventh draft of my life story. I sent the book I translated about ancient Aryan calendars to a publisher in Tehran a year after I arrived in Australia, but it was confiscated by the intelligence service. During my first three years here I wrote another book in Farsi about the aphorisms of Khalil Gibran, and then sent it to a different publisher in Tehran. They decided to publish it, but later told me the book had been banned by the government. I accepted that if I wanted people to read my work, I'd have to write in English.

My other hobby is inventing things. In 2001, after the anthrax attacks in New York, I invented a gloved bag that could hold any envelope and stop the spores from spreading. I contacted a marketing company in Melbourne, who volunteered to find a manufacturer for it. But two months later they discovered an invention identical to mine being produced by a French factory. I also developed an electric kettle that boils water in thirty seconds, three times faster than conventional ones, as well as a device designed to prevent drowning, a major cause of accidental death in Australia. Drown Alert is patented with IP Australia.

But my greatest efforts have gone into creating a generator that produces clean electricity. In early 2016 I finally succeed in building a prototype and sign a contract with a major manufacturer in Australia. I'm excited about what I believe is a breakthrough in energy technology and the possibility that it will replace fossil fuels as our major source of power. Creating the generator has taken up most of my free time, and my home in Tea Gardens has turned into a laboratory.

The ancient fig at the front of the house reminds me of the fig tree in front of our shanty house when I was a child. I used to sit under its kind shade and slowly eat a wafer I'd bought with money given to me by my father. Ah, my beautiful fig tree, forgive me for not having a chance to say goodbye to you. When I stand on my large balcony overlooking the Myall River, and observe the water glistening in the moonlight, I remember the river in Çankiri. But this time I'm not a homeless asylum seeker, starving and scared, struggling with poverty and pain; I'm not an *evsiz*. I have crossed the river. I am a free man now.

In late 2011, twelve years after I last saw my mother, she rings me with some exceptionally good news. She sounds joyful, a tone I haven't heard from her since I left Iran.

'Guess what, Kooshyar jan? I've got my passport back! The intelligence service contacted me last week and said I could have it. Now I can come and see you and Newsha and Niloofar!' She bursts into tears. Most Iranians own passports, even if they don't plan to leave the country in the near future, but MOIS confiscated my mother's when they arrested her just after I escaped and never returned it. What she has told me doesn't make sense, though. It seems unlikely that MOIS would allow my mother to join me in Australia, as they may want to use her again as a hostage to silence me. But I put aside my suspicions – there's nothing I can do about them anyway – and focus on the fact that I'll see my mother again.

'They contacted me last week and said I can have my passport back. Now I can come and see you and Newsha and Niloofar!' She bursts into tears.

The next morning I apply for a visitor visa for my mother. It's a complicated process, with a significant amount of paperwork, and will take a few months to complete. My mother now calls me every week to see whether there's been any progress. She's waited twelve years and feels she can't wait any longer.

The following week, when I'm walking home from work, my mobile rings. It's Mrs Azad from Caravan Publications in Tehran. I'm very surprised to hear from her – the last time was more than seven years ago. She tells me they've been given permission to publish my book about Khalil Gibran, and it will be in bookshops in less than three months. The approval was sudden, she says, and she doesn't know why it was granted.

Later on I receive ten copies of my book *Avaye Gibran*, the best writing I've ever done in Farsi. I'm ecstatic to see a new book with my name on the cover, and I wish I could be in Iran to see it in the shops.

In early 2012 I finish the final draft of my life story and submit it to a publisher in Melbourne. Their response is wonderful: they're very excited about the book and want to publish it. It's the best news, but something is niggling at me. All this luck seems too good to be true. I'm scared something horrible will happen. If fate knocks me down again, I don't think I'll have the power to stand up.

After months of correspondence and sending fifteen thousand dollars to Canberra as a surety against my mother staying in Australia for longer than three months, I'm told she must go to the Australian embassy in Tehran. After a brief interview she's finally granted a visa. I send her some money to buy a return ticket. She'll be here in four weeks. Newsha and Niloofar are thrilled.

A week before she arrives I speak to an Iranian friend, Bijan, who is a mortgage broker. He tells me he has a house for sale in Gordon, on the North Shore in a very nice part of Sydney.

'But I don't have any savings,' I tell him.

'Leave that to me. You have a great credit rating and a good income.'

The day of my mother's arrival comes. It's six-thirty in the morning and I'm at the airport; the plane lands in less than half an hour. My heart is thumping. She's been ringing me every day for the last three weeks in anticipation. 'I can't believe I'll see you,' she tells me. 'My entire life shattered when you left. I've been in a very dark place till now.'

Every minute I check the list of arrivals, in case she's early.

Newsha and Niloofar are next to me, Newsha holding a bunch of flowers and Niloofar with a card in her hand. Niloofar has no memory of my mother but Newsha remembers her very well. Azita would never come to see my mother; she hated her from the beginning. I haven't told my mother we've separated as I'm afraid her weak heart wouldn't take the shock.

'I've never forgotten the tale she told me of the little boy and his pigeons,' Newsha says excitedly. 'You know, the one about the lonely boy who works hard and saves money so he can buy a special pigeon, and this pigeon becomes his best friend. He's so happy until one day he finds that his pigeon has gone . . .'

As she's talking I realise that it's my story. My father heartlessly sold my beloved pigeons for a few coins. I tell Newsha, though, that it's just a fairytale.

'Look, Dad, here they come,' cries Niloofar, pointing. A group of passengers is walking down the ramp and most of them look like Iranians. We search for my mother, checking every woman in the crowd. Minutes slowly pass, and then I see an old lady limping towards us. Another woman walks past her but she's too young and tall to be my mother. The old lady stops and looks around.

'Is that Maman?' asks Newsha.

'No,' I say.

The old lady glances in my direction and her face opens into a big smile. She starts walking towards me more quickly. When she gets closer I finally recognise her beautiful eyes – and my heart aches. My mother has aged so much. I race up to her and pull her sleeve. Newsha and Niloofar run after me with the flowers and card. My mother's trying to say something, and to smile, but tears start running down her cheeks.

'Maman,' I whisper and hug her so tightly I almost crack her ribs. I hold her and cry and cry, remembering all those years of poverty, pain, fear, loneliness and sacrifice. During all those hard times she never gave up. My mother is my hero. I have my faith and my sanity, my passion and my courage from her. She gave me my identity.

Newsha touches my shoulder. 'Dad, people are looking at us,' she whispers in my ear. I finally let go and look around. She's right.

'Salam, Maman jan,' says Newsha, beaming as she gives her grandmother a hug. She's now taller than my mother is. I introduce Niloofar.

'Ah, look at you, gorgeous angel! You've grown so much. When I saw you last you were only a month-old baby!' My mother cries and holds Niloofar against her chest, rocking and whispering prayers in Hebrew.

When we get into the car my mother says worriedly, 'This must be very expensive.'

'Yes, Maman jan, but I'm a doctor now. I can afford a decent car,' I say.

'Where are we going?' she asks.

'It's a surprise.'

An hour later we're in a fancy hairdressing salon in Turramurra. I say to the hairdresser, 'My mother has come to visit us after twelve years. As you can see, her hair is all grey and I want her to look younger. I will pay for it, whatever you think is appropriate.'

The hairdresser smiles. 'Okay, I understand. Where's she from?'

'Iran.'

'She doesn't speak any English?'

'I'm afraid not.'

'That's fine. I'm from Greece – whenever my mother comes to visit she does the same thing, so don't worry about anything. Leave it with me.'

Newsha, Niloofar and I sit in the waiting area, watching.

'Kooshyar jan, I don't really need this. It's going to cost a lot,' my mother says.

'Please don't worry, just stay there and let her do her job.' But I know my mother. I've never seen her wearing any real makeup, except for on New Year's Eve when she'd wear the one lipstick she owned, which a friend gave her.

The hairdresser starts and my mother tries to ask her something. They're gesturing with their hands and fingers, indicating numbers to each other. Suddenly my mother yells out, 'She says it's going to be two hundred dollars!' and begins to climb out of the chair.

I rush over to her and ask her to sit down again. 'Maman jan, please stay there. It's going to be twenty dollars, I promise.'

'No, I know you're lying to me. I really appreciate the thought but I don't want you to spend that much money on me – you should save it for your daughters.'

'Maman jan, please, I beg you.' The hairdresser is laughing, and my mother submits. The whole process takes more than two hours, and every five minutes she wants to flee. But in the end I win.

I pay with a card so my mother can't see how much it really is but she demands to know, standing there with beautifully blow-dried brunette hair and subtle makeup. She looks twenty years younger.

'It was twenty-five dollars,' I say, staring at the ground.

'Look into my eyes and tell me,' she orders. I do – she can still scare me.

'Okay, I lied. It was thirty dollars.'

'Stop lying to me!'

'It was forty dollars,' I mumble.

'I said look at me!' I turn my head and look into her eyes.

'You haven't changed at all.' And she smiles. 'Okay, I'll let you go but next time I'll take my slippers out and teach you a lesson.' She says it just as she did years ago when I did something naughty, which was almost every day.

We drop Newsha and Niloofar at Azita's house and my mother and I drive another two hours to Tea Gardens. On the way I explain that Azita and I have separated. She's not as shocked as I'd feared; in fact, she's relieved, and she tells me she's been expecting this for many years. She is very supportive and only concerned about the children.

That night we sit up till late and talk about the past. When I finally ask about her arrest she falls silent and tries to hold back tears. I know she's afraid to talk about the ruthless treatment she suffered because of me.

'Maman jan, stay here. Stay in Australia with me. I'll look after you,' I tell her.

'I don't know.' She sighs, then opens her luggage and takes out a box, which she gives to me to open. It contains two books, my best friends during those dark nights in our decrepit slum. One, with a blue cover, is the Old Testament and the other, with a green cover, is a collection of classic Persian stories. I pick up the stories and hold it in front of my nose. The smell of the paper takes me all the way back home and unearths so many memories, mostly of nights when I was a frightened child and my mother read me the stories. They're wonderful presents, and I hug her.

Over the next three weeks I work five days a week instead of six, and on the weekends we drive to Sydney to see my daughters in the Baulkham Hills house. Bijan calls to say that my home loan has been approved, and my offer on the house at Gordon has been accepted. Before long he gives us the key for the new house, which has two storeys with four bedrooms and three bathrooms, as well as a massive backyard full of trees.

Having it means so much to me as now Newsha and Niloofar can stay with me in a house instead of me being alone in a hotel when I visit Sydney.

'Thank you, my Adonai,' I whisper.

My mother is delighted too. Then she adds sadly, 'I knew that your marriage would fall apart one day, but it still breaks my heart. It's my fault. I should've let you marry Mahshid, the girl who loved you. You and Azita had nothing in common. You must hate me for it. I can imagine how miserable it's been for you over the years.' She looks at me seriously. 'You must find love, Kooshyar. You work so hard and come home to nobody. You need to have someone in your life.'

I tell her that my family days are over, but she isn't convinced. 'Remember what the Torah says: "Man plans, God laughs!" You're still young. There are many nice people in the world, and I'm sure you'll find the right person.'

I go to work in Tea Gardens while my mother stays in my small house there, cleaning and cooking and washing. I know her: she can't stay still. Late one afternoon I go to the waiting room to call the next patient and see my mother sitting there. She says she was bored and lonely at home so she started walking to the medical centre, limping along with her sore knee, when a car stopped nearby. 'I gave her a lift,' explains Robert, one of my patients, a very nice man in his late sixties.

'He speaks French so we were able to communicate,' says my mother, looking pleased. Since she arrived her biggest issue has been the language barrier. The school she attended in Isfahan was run by the French government for Jews in Iran. That was where she learned French, and she still remembers it.

'Her French is so much better than mine,' says Robert, smiling.

In May we move to the new house in Gordon, spending weekends there and weekdays in Tea Gardens. The weather is getting cold and I take my mother to buy warm pyjamas in Kmart. I find a pair for ten dollars but she tells me they're too expensive, saying she can live on that amount for a month. She refuses to let me buy any clothes for her. However, when I come home from work one afternoon she's wearing a very fancy pair of pants and a trendy blouse.

'Look how nice they are,' she says in excitement. 'And they cost me three dollars!'

'Is that all? What was the shop called?' I ask.

'Viniz or something like that,' she says. I realise she's found the St Vincent de Paul shop. I smile and say, 'That's so you, Maman jan.'

While she's been here I've been eating proper food instead of the meat pies, sausage rolls and hamburgers I've been living on for seven years in hospitals. For the last two and a half months I've had wonderful Persian dishes every night. Nothing tastes as good as one's mother's cooking.

One night, after we finish eating a delicious stew, she says sadly, 'Kooshyar jan, I have to go back to Iran. My visa expires in two weeks.'

'You should stay with me. You don't have anyone in Iran.

I can apply for a bridging visa for you,' I say, desperately trying to persuade her.

'No, I don't know the language and it'll be too hard for me. I don't want to be a burden for you. I'm working as a bookkeeper for a big company in Iran – they're paying me well.'

'Maman jan, I *want* you to stay, so you can help me look after Newsha and Niloofar. I need you.' I'd become used to my desolate life before she arrived but having someone to talk to now and share my feelings with means I'll be lonely when she leaves, and I can't bear the thought. But my mother is an independent woman. She will not live in a foreign country and be a burden to me.

I tell her I've been writing a memoir describing what the Islamic regime has been doing to its citizens, to Jewish people, to other minorities and to women. 'When this book gets published the government will be furious. They might do something to you, just to put pressure on me. I'm so worried about you.'

'I'm a tough woman, Kooshyar jan. Go ahead and get your book published. I'll be fine.' I hope she's right.

On my mother's last night in Australia she cooks my favourite meal: lamb stew with celery and rice. The smell takes me back thirty years to when I was a naughty little boy and would run into the house starving. As I eat it now I wonder how I'll cope after she's gone. I want to see her all the time and feel her presence. I wish I could convince her to stay somehow. But it's not possible.

Finally we retire for the night. I lie down in bed and shut my eyes but I can't sleep. Suddenly the door opens and my mother's in the doorway.

'Can I come in?' she asks.

'Of course, Maman jan.' I try to sit up.

'No, just lie down.' Then she sits down next to my bed. She has the green book in her hand and she starts reading me my favourite story, 'The Little Black Fish'. It's about a tiny river fish that wanted to leave her parents and friends and find out about the ocean. My mother reads in the soothing voice she used when I was a child. I listen and pretend I'm falling sleep. I can feel my warm tears on the pillow.

It's cold and grey when I take my mother to the airport for her flight back to Iran. I'm not sure whether I'll ever see her again and I cannot bear to let her go. She whispers a Hebrew prayer and blows on my face.

'Adonai protects you,' she whispers. 'You will find love and start a family again.'

Then my mother walks away, leaving me lonelier than ever.

EIGHTEEN

In July 2012 the publisher rings from Melbourne to say my book is about to be released. I'm elated. The memoir covers my life from birth until I fled Iran. It's satisfying to have my words in print, but I know the book will jeopardise my safety and that of my mother.

I soon learn how carefully the regime has been keeping a check on my life. My email account has stopped working so I have my computer examined for viruses. The IT expert rings me and asks, 'Are you using your email now?'

'No, I'm at work.'

'I'm looking at your computer now. It definitely has a virus but what I don't understand is how someone has your email open right now.'

'Someone's checking my email?'

'Yes, it seems your emails are being intercepted,' he says.

He advises me to open a new account, which I do. I gather that the previous one stopped working only when I received or sent an email to a publisher or an organiser for a book event.

It all makes sense: the regime giving permission for my Khalil Gibran book to be published, and returning my mother's passport so she could visit me. Why? Because they know my memoir is going to expose their treatment of its citizens and they want to say, 'Dr Karimi is a free man; we haven't done anything to him. His mother is free too and has visited her son in Australia. We also let Dr Karimi's book be published in Iran, so anything bad he says about the government is rubbish!'

Yes, my Gibran book was published. But I can't forget when a young university student named Neda Agha-Soltan was demonstrating in the streets of Tehran with thousands of her colleagues. The Iranian forces opened fire and she was shot in the chest. She collapsed right in front of the Caravan office. Dr Arash Hejazi, their chief editor and a medical doctor, tried to save her without success. Someone filmed the entire event on a mobile phone and put it on YouTube.

The next day the footage was seen all over the world. Neda became an icon for Iranian women and the new movement for reform in Iran. Hejazi, who did nothing except try to revive her, was pursued by intelligence agents. He managed to escape to England, was interviewed by CNN and the BBC and gave evidence about Neda. The regime denied the whole thing. Caravan was shut down and my book was given to a different publisher, Kondor Publications. It sold more than four thousand copies, and I told the publishers to give the royalties to my father.

Despite his many faults my father has always held a special place in my heart. I remember when I was fourteen he came home from work, had a couple of shots of his homemade vodka and said he wanted to give me some advice. It was the first time he'd expressed a desire for serious conversation with me, and I was excited.

'A man must do three things in his life, Kooshyar,' he said. 'The first one is fight. The second is gamble. And the third is go to jail – it's where real men are formed.' At the time this perplexed me, but thirty years later I realise I have, in fact, done very well with my father's advice. I've fought passionately against an oppressive regime. I've gambled – not with cards, but with my life, in my fight for freedom. And I've gone to jail for it. All this would surely be enough to make my father proud of me.

On 12 August 2012 Wild Dingo Press launches *I Confess: Revelations in Exile* at the Melbourne Writers Festival. The book's dedicated to Habib Elghanian, an entrepreneur and philanthropist who in 1979 was the first Jew to be executed after the Islamic revolution. There's a large crowd at the launch and soon I'm invited to interview after interview. Every time a reader asks me to sign their copy I feel proud and pleased. The majority of the Jewish community in Sydney, Adelaide and Melbourne are supporting the book.

Meanwhile, my reputation as a doctor has been building in Tea Gardens, thanks to a few special cases. One afternoon in December 2011 a woman and her husband, in their early sixties, came to see me at the surgery. The woman had woken up that morning feeling very nauseous and had vomited once. 'I've got food poisoning,' she told me.

When I pulled up her shirt to examine her I noticed a few red spots on her stomach, and she told me they'd just appeared. I checked the rest of her but there was no rash anywhere else. The spots disappeared when I pressed on them but her temperature was a worrying 38.2 degrees.

She reluctantly let me give her an injection of penicillin, and I typed a letter of referral to John Hunter Hospital's emergency department in Newcastle. They protested, saying they were just visiting Tea Gardens and when they returned to Sydney they'd go to a hospital there. But I insisted.

They shook their heads and walked out obviously dissatisfied. I hadn't mentioned the frightening term 'meningococcal infection' to them but I'd written in my letter that I was concerned that's what it was. The disease can kill in less than four hours, and because it's endemic in Iran I easily recognised the symptoms.

The following afternoon I received a phone call from a specialist doctor at John Hunter Hospital. They'd diagnosed the woman with a viral infection, but a test had revealed meningococcal bacteria in her blood. 'We've asked her to go to Sydney Adventist Hospital immediately. She's on intravenous antibiotics now and she's going to survive, but if you hadn't given her the penicillin she would almost certainly have died,' said the doctor. A month later the couple came to see me with a big box of chocolates and a bottle of red wine to say thank you. The story had also spread around town, reinforcing the community's faith in me. To me the people here and in the surrounding towns are not just my patients; they're like my family. Without them my life would be meaningless.

Shortly after the book launch, I arrange to give a talk about my memoir in the local town hall. Almost everyone in the area has read it and every day at my surgery I sign copies. It's six in the evening and I have to be at the hall in an hour. I decide to call my mother as I haven't heard from her in a few days, but she doesn't answer. I ring her sister Nosrat, who also doesn't answer, but her other sister, Soraya, tells me my mother is in a small town near Isfahan for a few days' holiday. 'She'll be back soon, she's fine, don't worry,' says my aunt.

But I can tell something is wrong from her tone. I ring my uncle Mansoor. He tells me a different story. 'They're repairing phone lines near your mother's house so her phone's not working. It'll be fixed soon, don't worry.' Now I am certain my mother's in danger.

I ring my friend Makan, who's a Muslim member of my monarchist party in Iran. He's a very smart man with contacts everywhere. Calling him is extremely dangerous but I have no choice. I speak to him using our code words.

'Salam, Makan. I'm Saeed, just checking the results of your test drive with the car.'

'The car was taken last week from the garage by the dealer. The same one who took your own car years ago,' he says.

'Okay, take care,' I say.

I hang up and put my head in my hands. My mother has been imprisoned again by the intelligence service. Her relatives in Isfahan must know but they're too fearful to say anything. I think about my mother, an old woman with bad joints and a cardiac condition, at the mercy of those brutal monsters.

By now it's time for me to go to the hall so I pull myself together and drive there. After forty-five minutes of talking and answering questions I decide to tell the audience about my mother. I know the intelligence service has taken her to silence me, but I will not be silenced. 'I would like to share some horrible news with you,' I say, and tell the story.

The response is overwhelming. People are highly sympathetic and want to do something – contact the authorities, blog, tell the media. I appreciate their help and ask them to stay calm. Over the next four weeks I contact many organisations and groups including the UNHCR, the Jewish community, women's rights activists and feminists in Australia, and PEN, an international organisation representing imprisoned or persecuted writers. At every book event, at every interview, I talk about my mother's arrest. I try to hire a lawyer in Iran but no one has the courage to defend her. She's not allowed to contact anyone in the outside world, and no one is able to communicate with or visit her. I'm not even sure she's still alive. I can't eat or sleep but I continue to publicise the book. I have to do this for my campaign against the regime, for the Iranian people, for my mother.

The Australian foreign ministry tells me twice that the government is trying to secure her release but I can't be optimistic. Though some Iranian politicians might be concerned about deteriorating ties with Australia, the extremist hardliners in the government wouldn't care about international relations. So many people in Iran are thirsty for Jewish blood. Amnesty International, the UN and others all promise to do something but still my mother is in prison. I can't concentrate. I don't know what to do. I even consider going to Iran on a fake passport, though I know that would be suicidal.

One evening, more than a month after my mother is imprisoned, my phone rings. It's my aunt Soraya.

'Kooshyar, good news! The intelligence service phoned to say I can pick up your mother tonight. She's free to go.'

'Are you sure?' I can't believe it.

'Yes, we'll ring you again as soon as she's released.'

I stay awake and at four in the morning my phone rings.

'Kooshyar jan, are you okay?' My mother's voice is weak and trembling.

'Yes, Maman jan. Are *you* okay?'

'Yes. It's a miracle but thank Adonai I'm still alive.'

'Are you sick, Maman jan?' I ask.

'I'm fine.' And she hangs up.

Over the next two weeks Aunt Soraya takes my mother to various doctors. She has treatment for her heart but refuses to tell me exactly what's happened.

After she's released, my mother is told she'll receive a letter summoning her to court in the near future. The intelligence service has never informed her of what she's accused of, and she and I are both anxious about what sentence she might receive. It could be anything from a ten-thousand-dollar fine to ten years in jail. They can fabricate evidence against her and lock her up to put pressure on me. My only hope is that they're swayed by their relationship with Australia.

During this time Makan rings me. Because I contacted him he's had to escape Iran. He's in Dubai and is about to travel to Malaysia but he needs help getting somewhere safe. I feel terribly guilty; he has done so much for me. Now it's my turn to help him. Malaysia is an Islamic country and is friendly with Iran. Iranians can visit without a visa and there are many extremist Muslims there. It's not a safe place for me, but I must go.

I get on a plane without telling anyone and land in Kuala

Lumpur at midnight. In the morning I buy a mobile phone to use while I'm there, and I ring work to say I'm in Sydney with my children for the next three days and ask them to cancel my appointments. I wear a cap and sunglasses at all times and stay at a different hotel that night. From a public phone I ring Makan to organise a meeting, using our coded words.

I arrive at the café at nine the following morning. I look around to make sure I'm not being watched, but everybody looks suspicious to me. When Makan finally appears he doesn't recognise me; it's been many years since we saw each other. I approach him and we decide to keep walking and talking, constantly alert in case we're being followed.

Makan has already found a people smuggler. He doesn't have time to go to the UNHCR and must leave as quickly as possible. I give him seven thousand dollars and go with him the following day to the smuggler, making sure he'll be safe. I wish him luck and then get on the next plane back to Sydney.

I never heard from Makan again. Though I can't be sure of his fate, I suspect he was either caught and sent back to Iran or he never reached his destination. Around that time, the news seemed to be filled with stories of boat tragedies. In July 2012 almost a hundred people died in two separate incidents, and on 27 October 2012, a few days after I left Makan in Kuala Lumpur, thirty-two asylum seekers drowned when their boat sank on its way to Christmas Island. When I heard this news I couldn't help wondering in despair whether Makan's kind act of bravery had led to his death.

NINETEEN

It's more than three years since I separated from Azita and moved to Tea Gardens. Newsha has passed her Higher School Certificate exams and is studying journalism. She and Niloofar, who's now in year 9, continue to live with Azita and spend weekends with me. I still financially support them and my ex-wife. This isn't because I'm legally required to – in fact, Azita and I agreed not to put the girls through the stress of a courtroom. I want to be responsible for my daughters until they're independent so as long as they live with their mother most of the time, I've decided to provide for all three of them completely.

My work is demanding and I enjoy it. But despite this, there's a vast void in my life. Some nights I feel extremely lonely and isolated.

In the early hours I drive out of town to relax and clear my head so I can eventually sleep. My daily routine in Tea Gardens seems tedious, and although I enjoy spending time with my patients I have to keep a professional distance from them. I feel I have no real friends. One night I decide to ring Asef, who's been sent to Norway with Soosan. I haven't spoken to him for more than five years, as we've both been too busy dealing with the difficulties in our lives. I'm nervous. When he finally answers, we're both so excited to hear each other's voices, but Asef tells me how sad, repetitive and unproductive his life is.

'They said at the beginning it would take years to learn the language so we shouldn't bother. My children are happy but my life feels so empty.' When I ask about Soosan he bursts into tears and I panic, thinking she might have died. No, she's still alive, but suffering from major depression. She's been admitted to hospital many times and right now she's in a psychiatric ward, where she'll stay for another five months.

'She's so homesick,' he tells me. 'Here it's night for six months followed by six months of daylight, and extremely cold. We haven't adapted very well.'

I decide not to whinge about my own troubles to Asef. I try to give him hope and courage, but I know how insurmountable his problems are. When we say goodbye I sit in a corner and stare at the wall. I remember our miserable days in Çankiri, our daily struggle to stay alive, to keep dreaming of a new start in a beautiful country. And what of our dream now? I grab my Star of David. I'm not going to give up.

In February 2013 I register to go to Afghanistan with the UN forces. I want to be in a war zone, among bullets and mortars, among the wounded and people who really need me. I have to leave this safe haven of monotony. I know my daughters need me but I can't bear my tedious day-to-day life anymore, and I'll be a better father to them if I go and do something else for a few months. In April I'm told I'll be sent there on 27 August to treat injured civilians and soldiers and also to train nurses and junior doctors; my years of experience in Emergency will be a great help in this. I haven't told anyone I'm going because I know I wouldn't be allowed to leave. I plan to simply jump on the plane and disappear but, once again, my destiny changes completely.

Early on 5 May 2013 I'm standing at the back door of the surgery talking to our new practice manager, Steve, about my schedule. 'I'm triple-booked and seeing more than seventy patients a day. You have to cut it back, Steve.'

'We only have four doctors, though, and you're the medical director. I'm trying my best but there are just too many patients.' Then he adds, 'We're going to have a locum with us for four weeks.'

'Four weeks isn't going to solve the problem,' I tell him.

All of a sudden a red four-wheel drive pulls over in the parking area and a tall blonde woman steps out. She walks over to us, says good morning, and enters the medical centre. I'm stunned by her beauty.

'Who was that?' I ask Steve in awe.

'That's the new locum. Her name's Misha Johnson.'

Later on, Misha comes to my room and we chat about the patients and how the practice operates. She tells me she's from Tasmania and has been working as a locum in remote areas for the last three years. When our conversation ends I'm impressed by her charisma and selflessness. I think, What a shame she's only here for four weeks.

On the Monday following my appearances at the Sydney Writers' Festival, I'm sitting in my room getting ready for my first patient when Misha appears in the doorway.

'Good morning,' I say.

She walks in and puts her hands on my desk. 'What an amazing journey,' she says, staring into my eyes. I don't know what she's talking about but my heart is jumping out of my chest. 'I started reading your book on Friday night and couldn't put it down until I finished it, on Sunday afternoon. I'm speechless!' She shakes her head.

I only manage to smile and murmur, 'I'm happy you like it.'

I soon hear a lot about the new locum, about how kind and down-to-earth she is and that she's an exceptional doctor. Very soon all the nurses love her, and she even gets the approval of the cranky administrative staff. It seems I'm the only one who hardly gets a chance to talk to her, because I'm so busy. One day Steve drags me to the tearoom to show me a newspaper article about *I Confess*. I'm warming up my awful two-day-old petrol-station hamburger when Misha walks into the room. I decide to stay longer in the tearoom; helping people can wait. Debbie, one of the nurses, asks her about Tasmania. Misha starts describing the beauties of her homeland with great passion and I try to take in every word, but I'm distracted by her lovely brown eyes and her brilliant smile. Each time she looks at me, my heart squeezes like a fist.

Debbie says to me, 'I was just telling Misha you eat a hamburger and Pepsi every day.'

Misha smiles and says, 'It's a shame. You work so hard you don't get a chance to eat proper food.'

Over the next two days I avoid going to the tearoom. I feel

embarrassed at the idea of eating my cheap oily hamburger in front of Misha again. But I desperately miss seeing her, even if it's only while chatting with the others. On the weekend I go to Sydney to be with my daughters as usual, but I spend the whole time thinking about Misha and her smile. While we're watching TV, Newsha says, 'Dad, you've been separated from Mum for over three years. I'm worried about you – your life is so lonely in Tea Gardens.' I do my best to pretend to my perceptive daughter that everything's just fine.

The next day, before driving back to Tea Gardens, I pick up some Persian food: tender lamb kebab and charcoal chicken marinated in saffron and lemon. These are my favourite dishes, but I don't eat them that night. I take them with me to eat at work.

Monday is a hectic day at the practice, with too many patients. Just before lunchtime, a sixteen-year-old boy comes in after he's had a skateboarding accident. He fell off and landed on his shoulder, and the right side of his brain is concussed. He walked to the medical centre with his father but I notice that his right pupil responds sluggishly to light. He's quite alert, though, and apart from mild pain on the right side of his head he says he feels fine.

'Are you coming for lunch?' yells out Karen, one of the nurses, from the other side of the medical centre.

'You go – I'll join you soon,' I respond. Just as I'm about to leave the boy he starts vomiting, and then very rapidly loses consciousness and starts having seizures. For the next fifteen minutes I sit on his chest, resuscitating him and trying to pass a tube down his throat. The entire medical centre swings into action and three nurses help me attempt to control the boy's seizures while we wait for a helicopter to arrive from Newcastle to airlift him back. His father is being counselled by Steve. Fortunately, after forty-five minutes of pumping oxygen to his lungs and injecting him with various medications, the boy is shifted to the helicopter alive.

I resume work straight after he's gone and miss lunch, again. At five I accidentally bump into Misha in the corridor. 'You did a great job today, Dr Karimi,' she says seriously. I feel flattered.

The next day I'm determined to see my patients quickly and have a half-hour break for lunch in the tearoom, but one of the receptionists tells me a young man with a large bunch of flowers is waiting to see Dr Johnson. He says he's her husband. I feel as if a gigantic rock is crushing my chest. I give my Persian food to Steve and Debbie, and lose my appetite for a couple of days. I start hating myself for being so immature and hasty in my feelings. I think, How could you be so stupid? If someone is that gorgeous and lovable, what makes you think she'll fall in love with you?

It's Friday again and I finish at five to rush back to Sydney. I'm feeling miserable, and even the thought of seeing my daughters doesn't raise my spirits. It seems nothing can uplift me anymore.

The next morning I go to a Persian grocery shop in Parramatta to purchase some spice and basmati rice. While I search the shelves a bearded customer is raging against the Australian government. 'They send their troops to Afghanistan and Iraq. They're killing our Muslim brothers and sisters!' His thick-lensed glasses are fogging from the intensity of his hatred.

'Take it easy, Haron,' says the shop owner, who is pouring pistachios into a plastic bag. 'Don't forget that if it weren't for Australia you'd be in jail in Iran now.' This Haron must be the loud-mouthed fanatic I've heard some of my Iranian friends here talk about. They say he's unstable and untrustworthy.

'I don't care, I would have gone somewhere else.' Haron is

waving his index finger, as is the habit of extremists around the globe. 'Australians are so ignorant. They don't know about the American plot to destroy Islam. Last week I wrote another letter to the prime minister, warning her about CIA plans to infiltrate Australian society and trigger a civil conflict between Muslims and Christians. The Jews have planned all this!'

I purchase my items and leave while Haron is still raving. The shop owner is mocking him but I've seen a frightening fire in Haron's eyes. A year and a half later I see him again – live on all the TV channels. This time his index finger is on the trigger of a gun aimed at hostages in Sydney's Lindt café.

The next week passes quickly and unremarkably. I try to stay away from Dr Johnson to protect my feelings but one Monday Debbie rings my room at work. 'Dr Karimi, we're in the theatre with Dr Johnson and we need your help, please.'

'I'll be there in a second.' My heart is racing. I almost rush my consultation with Vinetta, a 72-year-old woman who is Tea Gardens' unofficial news station and one of my most loyal patients. People say the Myall River's tides wouldn't turn if Vinetta said they shouldn't.

'I see you have to go help Dr Johnson,' she says with a cheeky smile. 'I won't hold you up.'

In the afternoon when I walk to my car Misha's waiting for me in the parking area, having finished work for the day. 'You must be exhausted,' she says sympathetically.

'I'm okay, thank you.' I'm trying to avoid her eyes.

'By the way, someone told me today that you appeared at the Sydney Writers' Festival. How was it?' she asks.

'Great.' I sound short and rude.

'I love reading true stories of people who believe in what they do,' she tells me. 'That's why I work as a locum. It's so rewarding to go to more remote areas of Australia and help desperate people. I don't necessarily enjoy working in comfortable cities.'

I finally ask the question that's been on my mind for some time. 'But how can you be a locum when your husband is in Tasmania?'

'My husband?' She seems surprised.

'The man who came to see you a couple of weeks ago.'

'Oh, that's my ex-husband. We separated four years ago but in the last six months he's been trying to convince me we should get back together again, which is never going to happen.' She shakes her head.

I'm elated by this news. Before she walks away she says, 'Thank you for helping me today.' I feel like I'm Neil Armstrong, walking on the moon.

But soon Misha's four weeks are nearly up. I'm desperate to see her properly before she goes but have no idea how to spend some time with her. And then I'm told that Vinetta is waiting for me with a package.

'This is for you, Dr Karimi. You need to eat proper food to stay a healthy doctor.' I open the box to find a cheesecake and strawberries, as well as rice cookies and blue cheese. Before Vinetta goes she says, 'Make sure you have it with your colleague. I've made a gluten-free one especially for her.'

I follow her advice. Misha and I are finally in the tearoom together, eating the delicious cake. Misha tells me she suffers from coeliac disease and can't have gluten. I'm not surprised that Vinetta already knew this.

'Do you have more books in the pipeline?' Misha asks while cutting a slice of the cheesecake.

'Yes. I always have a few in my drawer.' I can't stop gazing at her stunning eyes.

'How do you get time to write that much?'

'I practise medicine with my left hand. I'm right-handed.'

Misha smiles. Before we go back to work she says, 'I've been here for more than four weeks and I haven't seen any part of this lovely town.'

'I can show you around,' I say, seizing the opportunity. I'm thrilled when Misha agrees and gives me her mobile number.

The following evening I'm sitting at home watching TV when suddenly my phone rings from a blocked number.

'Kooshyar jan, how are you?' My mother's soothing voice delights me instantly. But she's phoned with a purpose in mind. 'How is your love-life? Have you found anyone?'

'It's not that easy, Maman jan.'

'But have you been looking?'

'Ah, sort of . . . It's difficult finding a soulmate, or even a close friend.'

'I want you to search harder. I'm ordering you to,' she demands, bossy as usual. 'You have to be happy in order to provide for your daughters. I'm sure happiness is right in front of you, my darling.'

After she hangs up I pour a glass of wine and walk out to the backyard to look at the sky. It's beautiful and clear and full of stars. I think about my mother's words and instantly Misha appears in my mind. I have her number. Should I send her a text? Maybe it's wrong to contact her this late, but then again I wonder what she's doing in this town by herself. Although I offered to show Misha around, I'm too shy to suggest it again now. I wouldn't know what to say in the text anyway. It'd be very embarrassing if she found it inappropriate because I'm her medical director. Besides, what's the point? She leaves in four days.

I go back inside and have another glass of wine. I try to ring Newsha but she doesn't respond – she's probably out with friends. Then I sit back on the couch and flick through the TV channels. There's nothing interesting on, just a Japanese horror movie with tiny subtitles. I turn the TV off and pick up a book, read a few sentences and feel even more dejected. I put it down again, turn off the light and try to sleep.

On my way home from work the following day I go to the liquor store and buy two cheap bottles of wine. After I've called my daughters I sit in front of the TV, but again I can't focus. I don't know what's wrong with me. My mother's voice comes back to me: 'happiness is right in front of you'. I look around and see unwashed dishes, dusty furniture, mould in the bathroom and a filthy carpet. But there is something else – in every room, in every corner. Misha. She'll be gone in three days. This is my last chance. I check the time: eight o'clock. It's certainly too late to show her around town.

I decide not to be so careful. I grab my phone and text her: *I have a bottle of wine and a couple of precious stories to share. Would you be interested?* I press 'send' and feel like I've sent a nuclear missile launcher to North Korea.

Time stops. I pace up and down. I start to become convinced she's found my text offensive. Suddenly my mobile phone rings. I pick it up to check the caller's name. Oh no! It's Kaveh, an extremely irritating friend who rings me four times a year to tell me how amazing his married life is. Why does he have to call me *right now*? I want to sharpen a pencil and stab Kaveh in the left jugular vein. Instead, I don't answer. When the phone chirps – the alert for a text – I think, This must be her! But it's Kaveh again, leaving a voice message. And guess what: it's about his married life.

I'm about to delete the message when the phone chirps again. It's a text from Misha. I almost drop the phone as if it's red hot. I stand there, frozen with doubt. What if she says no? Or worse, what if I see her tonight and fall in love? I pull myself together and open the message: *That would be lovely. I'm at 12 Bennet Street.*

I'm ecstatic. I put on aftershave and my best shoes, grab the wine and almost run to the car. I turn on the engine, close my eyes and whisper a prayer to my Adonai. When I reach the address, I see lights on the second floor of an apartment building and a woman's silhouette on the balcony. My heart speeds up. When I knock on the door, Misha appears. Even if this is the only night we spend together, I'll be so grateful.

We go upstairs – she walks, I fly. I can hear mellow music, and her jasmine scent is intoxicating. She's wearing a beautiful pink top and blue jeans, and her hair cascades to her shoulders like golden silk. We sit on the balcony and talk about work, and then about our personal lives. She's so glamorous but at the same time so friendly I feel we've known each other for years. We keep talking past midnight and open the second bottle of wine, but neither of us feels fatigued.

'And how did you end up here, in Tea Gardens?' I ask her. She explains that after her marriage broke up she worked as a locum GP in far north Queensland and Western Australia, mainly in Aboriginal communities. Then she saw the position for here. 'I had no idea what it'd be like but the name of the town attracted me, as I've loved tea all my life. When I realised it was a small coastal town, I thought I'd give it a go.' A gentle breeze lifts her hair. 'It was an absolutely random decision.'

I gaze at her, delighted. That's exactly how I chose Tea Gardens as well. My best childhood memories always involve cups of tea.

Then she asks me about my life in Iran. I share my memories with her – some entertaining and funny, others gruesome or heart-breaking. More than anything, though, she wants to know about my life in Turkey as a refugee. She's very supportive of multiculturalism and asylum seekers.

'You've certainly had an interesting life, Kooshyar,' she says. 'You're a survivor.'

I look at the time: it's three-thirty in the morning. 'I'd better leave you alone now. We both have to work in a few hours. Thank you for having me. I've loved it – you have a kind heart.'

'My pleasure. I've thoroughly enjoyed every minute,' she says.

I go home but can't sleep; I'm still thinking about Misha. When she leaves in three days I'll be devastated.

The next day I'm too swamped with patients to meet up with her at work, and when I go home I badly want to see her. But yet again I'm plagued by doubts and negative thoughts, and by nine o'clock I still haven't contacted her. I'm afraid she'll think I'm a pest. Plus, she must be exhausted from last night so she's probably already in bed anyway. Eventually, though, I get the courage to pick up my phone and write a text: *How is your night going in this quiet, beautiful town?*

Suddenly my phone makes a sound. *I was waiting for you to contact me. Last night was the most amazing night in my entire life. I loved every piece of our conversation. It would be so lovely if you visited again.*

I read her words again and again. Then I run around like a

madman, putting on the wrong shoes and spraying aftershave in my eyes. In less than twenty minutes I'm at her place. This is when I realise I've forgotten to bring wine.

When Misha appears she opens her arms and gives me a warm hug, and all my anxiety falls away. We sit on the balcony again, listening to music and drinking and chatting. I enjoy every word she utters, every breath I take in her presence, every time she looks at me with those astonishing eyes.

After she's asked me more about my life in Iran, she throws me a difficult question: 'Would you go back one day, if the government changed and you were safe there?'

'I don't think so.' I can see my answer surprises her. 'Australia is my home.'

Then I ask how her family came to be in Tasmania. She takes a deep breath and looks up at the night sky. 'It all started because of a crane,' she says.

Her English grandfather, Bill, joined the British Navy when the Second World War broke out and was sent to the Indian Ocean. After a few months there a huge crane on one of the ships broke down. Nobody had experience in this kind of work except Bill, and he was promised a reward if he could fix it. They sailed to Hong Kong and while his shipmates enjoyed the bars there, Bill worked on the crane and eventually succeeded in repairing it. Unbeknown to him, a man from a large Australian engineering company was watching. As Bill prepared to return to England this man approached him, saying that his company was building an enormous crane in Burnie, Tasmania, and needed a supervisor. They offered Bill a large salary and promised to organise a visa for his pregnant wife and bring her to Tasmania. The transfer took a very long time, and when the couple were reunited their young son, Andrew, was eighteen months old. When the crane was finally finished Misha's grandfather had fallen in love with Tasmania and decided to stay there. Twenty-two years later Andrew married Linda, his first girlfriend, and they had two daughters, Sama and Misha.

'It's amazing, isn't it?' says Misha with a smile. 'You've come here from one side of the world and I'm from the other. Now we're sitting together on this magical night, sharing our stories.'

When I'm about to go, again at about three in the morning, Misha asks, 'What are you doing tomorrow night?'

'Missing you,' I whisper.

'I can't stay, Kooshyar. I have to go back to my family,' she says with a small sigh.

'I'm going to Afghanistan in eight weeks,' I tell her. 'A friend in Kabul has organised my trip.'

She's startled. 'Afghanistan? *No!* Why? Haven't you been through enough?'

'It's hard to explain . . . My life here is quite empty, Misha. I have to go.'

She's quiet for a moment, deep in thought. 'No, this community needs you. If you leave, the whole medical centre will collapse.'

'I know, Misha, but I really can't bear this tedium anymore. I'm a pacifist, yes, but not a conformist.'

She looks upset and, boldly, I step forward and hug her. I feel her arms on my back and her warm body soothes my heart.

I whisper in her ear, 'Thank you, Misha.' I'm incredibly sad she'll be gone soon, but at least I've found love.

*

It's been two weeks since Misha's departure. Fourteen days of heartache. Fourteen nights of deep loneliness. But she's changed something in me. I realise that though I loved Australia dearly before I met her, Misha has made me feel like I belong here. I consider the values and culture that shape Australia to be my own, and I don't feel detached anymore. I'm a proud Australian now, even if I never see her again.

On this evening I'm at home watching the news. It's as depressing as usual: more devastation, more violence, more death in Afghanistan, Syria and Iraq. I fly to Kabul in six weeks but I still haven't told anyone at work I'm leaving. I'm trying to minimise the number of people who know I'll be in Kabul for security reasons: I'll be an easy target there for the Iranian regime. If I do die, it will be sad for my children and my patients but I will embrace it. I almost want the bullets to pierce my chest, so my agony will disappear.

I pour a glass of chilled white wine and start drinking it when there's a knock on the door. I glance at the clock. It's seven-thirty. Who would visit me now?

The knocking resumes. As soon as I open the door I'm transfixed. It's her. She's come back.

'I love you, Kooshyar,' Misha says softly.

I hold her tightly in my arms. 'I love you, Misha jan.'

'What does "jan" mean?' she asks.

'It means "dear" in Farsi. That's the only Persian word you'll ever need to know, and you are my Misha jan forever.'

Misha has shown me love, something I've never experienced before. It's like discovering a beautiful secret room in an old house.

One night three months later, as we're returning from a walk by the river, I stop under the fig tree in front of my place. The large ivory moon is covered with mist like a dusty antique coin, and the hint of moisture in the air touches my face like a butterfly's soft wing. I kneel down and propose to Misha. I've never before asked a woman to marry me, and my heart is pounding in my trembling chest.

Misha's face brightens in the moonlight. She stands me up and holds me in her arms. 'I'm yours, Kooshyar jan,' she says.

We get married, something I hadn't dared dream of doing again. To me it's much bigger than surviving prison in Iran, or even getting out of Turkey. I used to dream in Farsi but since living with Misha I dream in Australian. The rivers are my rivers; the mountains are my mountains. I am at home again.

But a year later, on a summer's night, I receive a phone call from Tehran. It is Parvin.

'Kooshyar, your father is sick,' she says, sobbing. 'He wants to speak to you.'

This is the moment I've always dreaded. I knew on the day I fled Iran that I would never see my father again. Misha notices how upset I am and comes over. I whisper to her what's happening. She puts her hand on my shoulder and urges me to speak to him one last time.

'Baba jan . . . I love you. I love you so much, Baba,' I murmur. I say it again, louder and with pride.

There's silence on the other end of the line. I can hear him panting, and his struggle to breathe cuts through my heart.

'I love you too, Kooshyar.' My father knows my name! He loves me! I feel exhilarated. I miss him so much. I want to fly through the phone cable and hug him, one last time. I want to smell the diesel on his shirt, and touch his broad shoulders.

I sit outside all night and cry till dawn. And my father goes. The next day Misha and I plant a tiny grapevine in a quiet corner of our backyard in his memory.

As I write these words on my computer our first-born daughter, Anna, now twelve months old, is sitting on my lap. I glance over at my ancient typewriter, which acts as a reminder of my responsibility to bring the voices of suppressed men and women in the Middle East to the world. I look at Anna's beautiful dark brown eyes that are so like her mother's and I think about destiny, how strange it is, how it has led me so far from the slums of Tehran. I am rich in every possible way. I'm close to my daughters – Newsha sitting for her final exams in journalism, Niloofar preparing for her HSC – and have at last found happiness. Little Anna is playing with the Star of David around my neck, the symbol that has been central to my destiny, my anchor through my darkest days. I say softly to her, 'One day you'll be wearing this, Anna jan.'

ACKNOWLEDGEMENTS

My deepest gratitude to Lynne Blundell, Robert Hillman and Jacqueline Kent for editing my manuscript. A great thank you to my lovely literary agent, Pippa Mason at Curtis Brown, for her incredible knowledge and experience, and her care for story. Very special thanks to Rebecca Bauert from Penguin, who polished the final script with her sharp eyes and incredible talent, as well as to Sonja Heijn for her thorough work. Also to Meredith Rose at Penguin, whose skills are phenomenal and invaluable. Sincere appreciation to Ben Ball, my marvellous publisher at Penguin Random House. Ben, if this book brings about any changes for the better, I will owe you that. To my beautiful wife: you have given me the world. And to my gorgeous daughters: you are my heart, and I am joyfully proud of you.